ATHABASCA'S

AN ETHNODRAMA ABOUT INCARCERATION

BY DIANE CONRAD

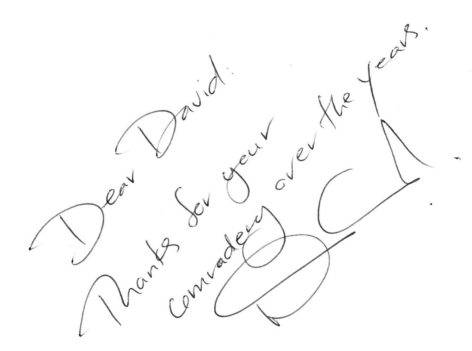

Dear David:
Thanks for your
comradery over the years.

SENSE PUBLISHERS
ROTTERDAM/BOSTON/TAIPEI

SOCIAL FICTIONS SERIES

Volume 02

Series Editors
Patricia Leavy
Stonehill College

The *Social Fictions* series emerges out of the arts-based research movement. The series includes full-length fiction books that are informed by social research but written in a literary/artistic form (novels, plays, and short story collections). Believing there is much to learn through fiction, the series only includes works written entirely in the literary medium adapted. Each book includes an academic introduction that explains the research and teaching that informs the book as well as how the book can be used in college courses. The books are underscored with social science or other scholarly perspectives and intended to be relevant to the lives of college students—to tap into important issues in the unique ways that artistic or literary forms can.

Please email queries to pleavy7@aol.com

International Editorial Advisory Board

"If you have come to help me you are wasting your time. But if you have come because your liberation is bound up with mine, then let us work together"

Aboriginal Activist Group,
Queensland, Australia 1970s

A C.I.P. record for this book is available from the Library of Congress.

ISBN: 978-94-6091-772-1 (paperback)
ISBN: 978-94-6091-773-8 (hardback)
ISBN: 978-94-6091-774-5 (e-book)

Published by: Sense Publishers,
P.O. Box 21858,
3001 AW Rotterdam,
The Netherlands
www.sensepublishers.com

Printed on acid-free paper

This work is dedicated to all youth across Canada who find themselves incarcerated in jails – and particularly to those youth with whom I had the privilege of working.

Shameful and indicative of systemic racism, is the disproportionate over-representation of Aboriginal youth amongst the numbers of incarcerated youth in this country. This is a human rights issue that demands all our attention.

The first production of *Athabasca's Going Unmanned* was February 17-19, 2010, written by Dr. Diane Conrad under the Canadian Actors' Equity Association Guest Artist Policy in association with the Canadian Centre for Theatre Creation, Department of Drama, University of Alberta, with the following cast and crew:

Wesley .... Sarain Waskewitch
Randy .... Cole Humeny*
Stan .... Richard Lee*
Eileen .... Darlene Auger
Jim .... Eric Nyland*
Val .... Melissa Thinglestad

Various (on video): Mari Sasano, Pamela Schmunk, Garett Spelliscy

Director: Ian Leung*
Dramaturge: Kim McCaw
Stage Manager: Dawn Friesen*
Cree language consultation: Darlene Auger
Fight director: Patrick Howarth
Production Designer: Daniela Masellis
Assistant Lighting Designer: Kevin Green
Videographer: Clinton Carew
Technical Crew: Amy Kucharuk, Matthew Latimer
Running Crew: Amy Kucharuk, Matthew Latimer

*Appeared with permission of the Canadian Actors' Equity Association

TABLE OF CONTENTS

ACKNOWLEDGEMENTS

My heartfelt thanks to all those individuals and organizations that helped make this project possible; without whom it would not have happened:

The Alberta Office of the Solicitor General and Edmonton Young Offender Centre for allowing me access to the institution.

Doreen Lesperance the Native Program Coordinator for allowing me to work with her Native program and for all her help and support along the way.

All the youth with whom I worked for their generosity in sharing their stories with me and for their willingness for us all to play together.

Darlene Auger and her associates for Cree and "Crenglish" translations.

Tyler Johnson for reading and advising on the play and Jesse Bayley for reading segments of the play and advising me on language.

Susan Spence-Campbell, Donna Krammer, Danielle Land, Michael Florizone, Lindsay Ruth Hunt, Alison Urban, Tai Munroe, Matthew "Gus" Gusul, Janine Plummer and Michael Coulis for their research assistantship on the project.

The Social Sciences and Humanities Research Council of Canada and the Canada Foundation for Innovation for funding the project.

The University of Alberta, Faculty of Education, Dept. of Secondary Education.

My colleagues and friends at the University of British Columbia who participated in a reading of the first draft of the play, and/or also read scenes for a presentation at the IDIERI conference in Sydney, Australia: Dr. George Belliveau, Jaime Beck, Amanda Wager, Graham Lea, Donnard MacKenzie, Vince White, Heather McDermid, and Hartley Jafine from York University.

Dr. Lynn Fels, Simon Fraser University and her class who read and workshopped scenes from an early draft of the play.

Derek Walcott and Conni Massing for reading drafts of the play and feedback.

The Department of Drama, Canadian Centre for Theatre Creation's Director Kim McCaw for his dramaturgical assistance; Ian Leung for his administration of the play's production and for taking on the role of the production's Director.

All the theatre artists involved in the play's first readings, workshops and production: Darlene Auger, Michele Brown, Ryan Cunningham, Richard Lee, Patrick Howarth, Cole Humeny, Jesse Gervais, Frederick Zbryski, Garett Spelliscy, Sheldon Elter, Melissa Thingelstad, Dawn Friesen, Eric Nyland, Clinton Carew, Daniela Masellis, Sarain Waskewitch, Mark Jenkins, Mari Sasano, Pamela Schmunk, Kevin Green, Amy Kucharuk, Matthew Latimer, also Arts on the Avenue, Larry Clark, the City of Edmonton, Michael Kennard, M.E. LaZerte High School, Christy Morin, and the Theatre Garage.

The Canadian Actor's Equity Association.

The "extras" who appeared in video segments of the production.

Michael Coulis for poster & program design, photography & video recording.

Dwayne Donald and Bev Bagnall for offering their advice on the play.

ACKNOWLEDGEMENTS

A special thanks to Elder Rose Wabasca for offering a smudge ceremony and prayer for opening night of the play's first production.

All members of the audience for the play's first production for their generous feedback and support.

Patricia Leavy for recommending this manuscript for her Social Fictions series.

INTRODUCTION

Athabasca's Going Unmanned is set in a youth offender jail in Alberta, Canada and tells the story of three incarcerated youth and the corrections staff who work with them. The story centers on an escape plot hatched by the inmates and ultimately examines the needs of incarcerated youth and the prospects for offering them programming with transformative potential. Based on extensive research with "at-risk" youth and incarcerated youth, the play addresses a range of real-world issues with sociological, criminal justice, policy and educational implications. Moreover, issues of race and ethnicity feature prominently.

The Play

The action begins on Val's (Caucasian female, 30) first day at her new job as the Program Director at the facility and spans over a two and a half month period. A week prior to Val's first day, a young man Randy (Métis male, 17) was admitted to the facility, charged with assault, awaiting trial. Other inmates include Wesley (Cree male, 17), in jail for matricide, and Stan (White or African or Asian-Canadian male, 16), a repeat offender. Other staff, whom we meet, include Eileen (Cree female, 40), who Val hires to run the Native and Drama programs, and Jim (Caucasian male, 30), another corrections staff member.

While the story progresses linearly for the most part, it jumps in time so we see only fragments of action. Interspersed throughout the play, disrupting the plot's linearity, are scenes in video (projected on a screen when performed live). These video scenes are alternative endings to the play – representations of the characters' fantasies or fears in relation to the potential escape plan that is the driving force of the play's action. The escape plan is initiated by the boys – primarily Wesley, but in which all the characters (except Jim) become implicated. Whether the escape plan is real – actually executed, successful or failed, performed or imagined remains ambiguous.

The alternative endings interspersed throughout are offered as possible outcomes to the potential choices the characters make. The audience is called upon to make sense of the ending for themselves. This deliberate ambiguity draws attention to the multiple performative possibilities and highlights opportunities for doing things differently. These alternative endings can be used in college courses as prompts for class discussions about a range of topics including but not limited to: juvenile delinquency, "at-risk" behaviors, the prisons system, socialization processes, race and ethnicity, rehabilitation and transformative educational programs.

Background Research

This play is based on my nationally funded participatory arts-based study entitled *The Transformative Potential of Drama in the Education of Incarcerated Youth* which was set within the Native program at the Alberta youth corrections centre. The study asked how applied theatre practices could contribute to the education of incarcerated youth to help them avoid future negative outcomes of their behaviours – through exploring the educational needs of incarcerated youth; devising practices that could contribute to meeting their needs; seeking possibilities for creating spaces within jail for transformative processes to occur; and through assessing the benefits of interventions in this context. Following the three years of weekly applied theatre sessions with incarcerated youth, with the aim to do so from the outset, I wrote the full-length ethnodramatic play.

My interest in studying the experiences of incarcerated youth was inspired by my previous research with "at-risk" youth in schools, who told me that for them, school was like a prison. Indeed schools and prisons can be seen as analogous, as Foucault suggests, in that both were founded as disciplinary bodies with the aim of normalizing individuals' conduct. Students or inmates, as objects of the power wielded in these institutions often respond with resistance – which may account for high drop-out rates for students and the high rate of recidivism amongst young offenders. Such dynamics are counter-productive to education aimed at personal growth and social development. If education can have a transformative impact, my study suggested, it must turn youth resistance from destructive to productive ends.

To this end the study sought educational practices through participation in applied theatre and other popular arts forms to turn youths' attention away from criminal activity toward possibilities for change, while problematizing taken-for-granted institutionalized practices. It aimed to critically analyze, with youth, the social structures that construct criminality, and to aid in the reconstruction of their roles and identities as other than criminal or deviant. The play also seeks to draw attention to the overrepresentation of Aboriginal youth in Canadian jails. Statistics confirm that Aboriginal youth in Canada are eight times more likely to be incarcerated than non-Aboriginal youth, suggesting systemic racism within the justice system that needs to be addressed. Parallels can be made to minorities in the US criminal justice system, with racial minorities disproportionately represented in that prison system as well.

While the play is fictionalized for dramatic effect and for ethical reasons, in some respects more evocative than realistic, the play's characters, settings, themes and plot are intended as an ethnographic re-presentation of the research – a creative expression of the research findings. The sources I drew on for creating the play included my researcher/facilitator field-notes and journals recording and reflecting upon my participant observations of the day-to-day lives of the youth within the context of the jail – notes on what they told me and the interactions amongst the group members, as well as notes and reflections on the processes of our creative work together; along with all of the artifacts from our three years of applied theatre work together including: youth devised drama scripts, transcribed stories, poems, digital photographs, digitally manipulated photos, digital stories, drawings, other visual art/craft works, and video recordings of dramas and other activities.

Live Performances

With assistance from the Canadian Centre for Theatre Creation at the University of Alberta, the play was professionally produced. The five performances of *Athabasca's Going Unmanned* drew a total of 250 audience members including academic faculty and students from education, drama and sociology, a number of corrections employees and many members of local Aboriginal communities, as well as community members at large. One matinee audience included sixty youth from two different schools including an inner city school and an Aboriginal reserve school. Each show was followed by a talkback period with the audience, and audience responses were overwhelmingly positive. The story seemed to resonate with people. Youth identified with the youth characters. Aboriginal audience members told me I had accurately captured aspects of their experiences. The laughter that the performances elicited indicated the successful portrayal of the humor of the characters and the situations. I managed to capture the reality of the context of incarceration as audience members who were corrections workers and youth who had been to jail said that the setting and characters were recognizable.

My aim in using ethnodrama as a means of disseminating the research was to engage a diverse audience with the research and to engender empathic under-standings of the experiences of incarcerated youth leading to more constructive attitudes regarding their needs. Performance has the potential to reach audiences in ways beyond intellectual understanding, through engaging other ways of knowing that are empathetic, emotional, experiential and embodied, with the potential for radically re-envisioning social relations. The same is true when using the written play in college courses. The fictionalized format invites students to engage with complex questions pertinent to their courses without relying on an "authoritative" text that closes off meaning-making. Rather, students are invited into the meaning-making process as they read and discuss the play and its alternative endings.

Teaching with the Play in College Courses

The play evokes a complex reality and a search for alternatives, for solutions to broad social challenges – alternative ways of thinking about and enacting youth justice. The ending of the play is left deliberately ambiguous with possibilities for both tragedy and comedy. While there are many comedic elements in the play – to represent the humor and laughter amongst the youth participants that was a regular feature of our work together, and to capture some of the quality of humor unique to Aboriginal culture, ultimately, the story of youth crime and incarceration is a tragic one. The play raises many challenging issues at the level of fantasy and imagination – an exaggerated reality, using symbol and metaphor, precisely in order to draw attention to and elicit discussion around these controversial issues.

The play is fraught with tensions and controversy as it asks:

– How can we do youth justice differently?
– How do we make change?
– What is the change we are looking for?

- What is needed to get there?
- What might an alternative look like?
- What role can applied theatre play?
- What are the challenges and pitfalls?

In the spirit of arts-based research and a "pedagogy of engagement", it arrives at no easy answers to these questions – rather, it acknowledges that answers will always be contextual and contingent. In this vein the play is a teaching tool for promoting critical thinking and creative problem-solving skills.

Given the subject matter of the play and the research that informs it, the book is an ideal supplemental text for courses in education, sociology, criminology/ criminal justice, theatre arts and arts-based research.

CHARACTERS

VAL White woman. 30-35ish. The newly hired Program Director for the youth jail.

EILEEN Cree woman. Mid-40s. Hired by Val to facilitate the Native program, art program and drama program.

JIM White male. 30ish. A security staff person at the jail.

RANDY Métis male. 17. Charged with assault linked to drug trafficking.

WESLEY Cree male. 17. Serving a juvenile sentence for killing his mother.

STAN White (or African or Asian) -Canadian male. 16. A repeat offender remanded for breach of probation.

    Various other characters as part of the video scenes: Amy (Wesley's girlfriend); news anchor; reporter; constable; Sergeant Smith; politician; people on the street being interviewed: young woman, elderly man, middle-aged woman, middle-aged man; other police officers; extras.

SETTING

Inside a provincial youth jail. The scenes take place: on the unit Athabasca; in Val's office; in Randy's cell; in the corridor. Interspersed are video scenes projected on screen.

TIME

Present day. The play begins on Val's first day on the job and spans over ten weeks.

PROLOGUE

Video on screen. (In the first production both the prologue and epilogue were show on a TV monitor – rolled on and off stage, to distinguish them from the "fantasy videos" that appear throughout projected on a wall-mounted screen upstage.)

Close up of an anchor person sitting behind a news desk in a studio. We hear the news jingle. A caption on screen says "Sask. police recapture last of six escaped inmates," along with an image of the outside of a jail with high brick walls and barbed wire fencing.

NEWS ANCHOR

News this morning of the recapture of the last of the six inmates who escaped last month from a Correctional Centre in Regina, Saskatchewan. 25 year old, Raymond, was taken into custody after a standoff on a Saskatchewan reserve last evening. Responding to a tip they received, police report they moved in on a home. Shots were fired, but no one was hurt. After several hours Raymond surrendered. Officials have indicated that, as well as standing trial for the original murder charges, Raymond, along with the other recaptured inmates, will face charges for escaping lawful custody. Here's Jamie Barrie with more.

Switch to a medium shot of a reporter on a city sidewalk speaking into a microphone.

REPORTER

This is Jamie Barrie in Edmonton, Alberta where news of the recapture of the last of the escaped Regina inmates was met with great relief. I'm here today to get the views of people on the street.

Switch to a series of shots of individuals being interviewed on the same sidewalk. All those interviewed are White and middle-class.

Switch to young woman.

YOUNG WOMAN

The whole incident was quite worrisome. I mean, they caught some of them in Manitoba. They could as easily have come here. I don't feel safe walking on the street knowing there are escaped criminals on the loose. Who knows what they were planning next? I could have been their next victim.

Switch to elderly man.

ACT ONE

ELDERLY MAN

Unacceptable. I can't believe authorities allowed this to happen. What sort of system are we running? They can't even keep hold of their prisoners? The six who escaped, most of them were young guys too. I ask you: What kind of lazy job are they doing? Can't keep watch of these young devils.

Switch to a middle-aged couple.

MIDDLE-AGED WOMAN

They need to be more proactive with these fellows. The paper said the prisoners themselves were surprised that they were able to get away with it. They had nothing better to do, so they just kept going ahead with the escape attempt . . .

MIDDLE-AGED MAN

Said the guards were even tipped off about the whole thing.

MIDDLE-AGED WOMAN

They ought to do activities with them, you know? Keep them occupied.

MIDDLE-AGED MAN

Forget that. Lock'em up and throw away the key. That's what I say.

Switch back to reporter.

REPORTER

And there you have it. Back to you Peter.

Switch to news anchor.

NEWS ANCHOR

We have this report from one of the officers at last night's arrest.

Switch to a medium shot of a constable at the scene of the arrest – outside a house on the reserve.

CONSTABLE

We're just happy that this situation has been resolved. Public safety was our primary concern and that has been addressed. Now that the inmates have been recaptured an RCMP investigation is underway. It will focus on accountability. How did they escape in the first place? Who helped them at the time of the escape and while they were at large?

Switch back to news anchor in the studio.

NEWS ANCHOR

We'll have an update for you on that story at noon. In other news, Malti a baby Asian elephant at the Calgary Zoo is gravely ill.

End of video.

ACT ONE

SCENE 1 - THE ESCAPE

A video is projected on screen. Each of the video scenes represents one of the characters' dreams, fantasies, or fears. Although Amy (Wesley's girlfriend) does not appear in the play as an actual character this video is Amy's fantasy. It is in DIY style and quality as though shot on a cell phone. (In the original production the three video clips were played back as though they had already been posted to YouTube – with the title "I broke my boyfriend out of jail".)

It is night. In the immediate foreground, at ground level entirely filling the scene, is a chain link fence – the video is shot through the fence. The videographer is a young woman, Amy, whom we see only briefly – her face, arms and legs as they move in and out of the moving camera frame, is close to the ground. In the distance we see three shadowy figures creeping slowly along the ground approaching the camera. We hear Amy's voice give out a little squeal. Three young men arrive at the fence – they are Randy, Wesley and Stan, who we'll meet again later in the play, inmates of a maximum security youth corrections facility. They are all dressed in identical navy blue sweat shirts and sweat pants. They arrive at the fence, still creeping close to the ground. We hear Amy's voice in a whisper . . . Close up on Wesley's face.

AMY'S VOICE

(An excited whisper) Wesley, you made it. You're here!

WESLEY

(Also whispering affectionately) Shhh. Amy. We're not out yet. *(He notices the cell phone)* What ya doin'? Put that away.

AMY'S VOICE

I'm recording it. To post on YouTube.

WESLEY

Don' have time for that. Gi'me the cutter.

In silence we see Amy's hand pass a wire cutting implement to Wesley through a space in the fence.

ACT ONE

WESLEY

(Commandingly) I said turn it off.

The cell phone camera shuts off and then comes on again – the action continuing after a break in real-time. The camera is in motion, so the picture is shaky. We see three shadowy figures creeping along the fence line – the three young men in a row with Wesley in the lead and the cell phone camera with Amy in the rear. We hear Amy's breathing. We catch glimpses of the high fence topped with barbed wire and the building ahead, trees and an open field in the other direction. In silence they creep past the side of a building and behind some pine trees where they all stop briefly. We hear more anxious breathing.

WESLEY

(In a whisper to Randy) Yo, ya got the key ready?

RANDY

(Also whispering) Got it.

WESLEY

Aight then.

We see Wesley's head and face move in toward the camera and Amy. We hear a small kiss.

AMY'S VOICE

(Soft and sweet) I missed you.

WESLEY

Said turn that off.

The camera goes off and then on again – with another advance in real-time. We see the inside of a car from the back seat. Randy is in the driver's seat. Stan is in the front passenger's seat. Wesley is in the back with Amy. Randy starts the car and moves through the parking lot. The three passengers crouch low in their seats as the car moves past the bright lights at the front entrance. We see a Canadian flag flapping atop a flag pole and part of a sign that reads Young Offender Centre. The car continues into the driveway. All are still silent and crouched. The car turns onto a dirt road. A few seconds on the dirt road the car speeds up and the mood changes dramatically. The passengers pop up in their seats. There are sighs of relief, back slapping, laughter and whooping. Randy turns on the car radio loudly and searches for music.

WESLEY

(Loud and jubilant) Ya, we made it!!! We made it!!!!

STAN

(In a celebratory tone to Amy) D'ya bring us smokes?

We see a cigarette package and cigarettes being distributed and lit as the laughter and whooping continues for a few seconds. The camera cuts out suddenly.

End of video.

SCENE 2 - NEW PROGRAM DIRECTOR

In the corridor. It is Val's first day in her new position as Program Director for the youth corrections facility. At the upstage end of a long corridor are a set of double doors with windows of reinforced glass. We hear a Pshshsht sound – the sound of a door unlocking. Val and Jim, joined by Eileen come through the doors into the corridor. Through the open door we catch a glimpse of others heading off in various directions. They are coming from the morning briefing where all administrators and staff assemble to discuss the day's goings on at the Centre: individual cases, issues, concerns, upcoming activities, etc. Val and Jim are both wearing corrections staff uniforms – button up shirts, black pants, black boots. They wear belts with two way radios on their hips. Val is carrying a bag over her shoulder and an armload of papers. Eileen is dressed in regular clothes. They are in mid-conversation as they enter the corridor together. The beginning of the conversation takes place just inside the doors.

JIM

(Calling out to others behind him also departing the meeting – Jim's farewell greeting) Watch your back. *(Then speaking to Val)* Police Chief Robertson's daughter, eh? Can't believe it.

VAL

Ummm. Did you know him?

JIM

No . . . No, before my time. But everyone speaks real highly of him.

EILEEN

I shook his hand once.

JIM

Good man.

VAL

(Ambivalent) Ya. Good man.

JIM

(Ready to head off to elsewhere) Well then. Have a good first day. Let me know if there's anything you need. *(Addressing Eileen matter-of-factly)* How's the Rez? *(With a little laugh and a gesture)* Managing to duck the bullets? Guess we'll be seeing more of you. *(As he begins to leave)* Watch your back. *(Calling to Val)* Best to button up, eh? *(Indicating the button at the collar of Val's shirt which is undone)*.

Jim motions to a person at a desk on the other side of the doors – a request for the door to be unlocked. Val immediately reaches for the top button of her shirt and tries to do it up with her one free hand.

VAL

Oh ya.

A Pshshsht sound and Jim exits through one of the doors leaving Val and Eileen alone in the corridor.

EILEEN

Wats'tagâc *(i.e. "Oh my god" in Cree)* Can you believe that? Duck the bullets?

VAL

(Still struggling with the button) Sorry. That was ignorant, wasn't it?

EILEEN

Never mind. Working here you need a thick skin.

VAL

You shouldn't have to put up with that.

Val puts her bag and armload of papers down to attend to the button with both hands.

EILEEN

I don't think you need to worry about the button.

VAL

He's got a point *(She finally gets the button done up)*.

ACT ONE

EILEEN

No, he doesn't. He always expects the worst from the kids. Maybe if he wasn't like that, he wouldn't always have to be watching his back.

VAL

Anyway *(Letting it slide, picking up her things)* . . . Thanks again for coming in today. When Shelly in admin said you'd been volunteering here over the years . . . And I remembered you from those workshops . . .

EILEEN

(Remembering) It was for a graduate course in criminology, right?

VAL

I knew I had to get you to come in to work with the kids.

EILEEN

These programs are long overdue.

VAL

I think they'll really help . . . Give them something productive to do and . . . get them thinking . . . about their behavior, about how to make change. I'd like to get things going right away. You're available to start?

EILEEN

Anytime.

VAL

Come to my office.

They begin walking down the corridor together.

VAL

(Excitedly) We'll go over details. I'd really like you to be here every day, but if that's too much? I've got lots of ideas. Oh, and a bunch of art materials, and stuff to make dreamcatchers . . .

At the "dreamcatchers" remark, Eileen gives a look of exasperation. Val, oblivious, keeps chatting as they exit together in the direction of Val's office.

SCENE 3 - VAL MEETS THE BOYS

It is a couple of days later on the unit called Athabasca. (All the units are named after Alberta rivers.) Throughout all the scenes on Athabasca, Val is constantly interrupted by the PA, the phone and the two-way radio she carries on her belt.

Val, Randy, Wesley and Stan are sitting on chairs in a circle in the middle of an open area of the unit. The space is empty and the walls are bare. It is afterschool "extracurricular" time. The boys are munching on cookies and drinking from small juice boxes. Wesley is cocky from the start. The others are sullen, but polite – becoming more animated as the scene progresses. As the scene begins they are in mid-conversation.

WESLEY

Word. Um? What's your name again?

VAL

Val. That's okay. It'll take some time for us to get to know each other.

WESLEY

(Continuing) Thanks for this, Val *(Indicating the juice and cookies)*.

RANDY

(Mumbling agreement) Straight up.

VAL

Like I was saying, I want to get Eileen in regularly. Stan, you said you met Eileen before?

STAN

(Between munches of his cookie) Ya. Think she was doing drumming. You were there, eh Wes?

WESLEY

Don't remember.

11

ACT ONE

VAL

Eileen has some Native cultural stuff she wants to do with you, and art and drama.

WESLEY

Drama? You mean actin'? Like on TV?

STAN

Like Dakota House?

RANDY

I saw him once at Q Club.

STAN

You did?

RANDY

Got stuck with a crappy table 'cause a some tournament he was in.

WESLEY

So what? What's that make ya?

Wesley and Randy glare at each other.

STAN

(Deflecting) He was in One Dead Indian.

VAL

(Bringing the conversation back to the program) Not exactly like on TV, but something like that.

Pause as the boys are finishing up their snacks. Wesley and Randy take furtive glances at one another.

STAN

Are we gonna have snacks every time? I'll come for snacks.

VAL

Does that mean you're interested?

WESLEY

Long as she don't make us do nothin' wack.

STAN

Here on Athabasca?

VAL

Yup. I'm thinking couple times a week and maybe something on weekends. Eileen wants to build a sweat lodge in the yard.

WESLEY

A sweat lodge here?

RANDY

What else? Any sports?

STAN

Can we still do basketball?

WESLEY

And hockey 'n weights?

VAL

We'll have those too.

STAN

What 'bout drawing? Can we do drawing? Can we make videos?

WESLEY

That'd be cool.

ACT ONE

VAL

Ya. Sure. We can probably work in some of that. And if you think of anyone else
who might want to join us . . .

STAN

I 'member her now. Told us those trickster stories that time. *(Nudging Wesley and
chuckling)* Man they were wacked. 'Member?

RANDY

(Insulted by trickster stories being called "wacked") What d'you know 'bout it?

STAN

(Apologetically) Jus' meant . . .

WESLEY

Leave'im alone. He's our fav'rite Windian *(a term for "White Indian" –
substitute with "Chindian" – Chinese Indian; or "Blindian" – Black Indian, etc.
depending on the race of the actor).* Aren't ya Stan?

STAN

(Proudly) Ya.

RANDY

Whatever . . . Windian *(or substitute).*

WESLEY

What're you suppos'to be? Don' look like any Indian I ever seen.

RANDY

(Angry) I'm Métis.

VAL

Cool it guys.

WESLEY

What the . . . ? He's the one talkin' crap.

STAN

Forget 'it.

RANDY

(Challengingly) And what?

Randy gets out of his chair and takes a step towards Wesley across the circle, who gets up. There's a brief standoff. When Randy turns to retreat, before Val can respond, Wesley kicks Randy's legs out from under him and Randy falls to the ground. Val leaps out of her chair.

VAL

Guys!

Stan goes to help Randy up. Wesley pulls his chair out of the way and sits down.

WESLEY

You saw that. I was defendin' myself. He came at me.

Randy tries to go for Wesley again, but Val steps in to hold him back. Val holds Randy by one arm.

RANDY

F'n goof.

Val places herself between the two boys. Stan stands aside. Wesley sits up in his chair defiantly.

VAL

Randy. Don't make me call code *(i.e. call for assistance)*. Geez you guys, I'm trying to run some programs here.

Pause. Wesley and Randy continue to glare at each other.

ACT ONE

VAL

(To Wesley) Go stand by the door. I'm taking you back to the unit.

WESLEY

No probl'm. Wasn't me trippin' like a little girl. All moody.

Wesley gets out of his chair and just before he turns to go to the door he takes a step forward around Val and lands a punch in Randy's gut. Randy recoils. Val supports Randy, still holding him by one arm and yells at Wesley.

VAL

Wesley.

Wesley moves quickly to the door followed by Stan. Val is still holding Randy by one arm.

VAL

(To Randy) Come'on. You're okay *(More a statement than question)*.

Val moves with Randy towards the exit door stopping at the communications console – the "pod." She presses a button on the pod and speaks into the speaker.

VAL

Door 200 please. Athabasca's going unmanned.

A crackly voice comes from the console: "You got it." A pause. Then the Pshshsht sound of the door unlocking. The lights go off as they push open the door and exit through it. They walk into the corridor.

VAL

(Ordering Wesley and Stan) Walk ahead.

Stan and Wesley walk ahead. Val follows with Randy, still holding him by one arm.

VAL

(Angry) You guys better get your act together if you want to do any programs.

WESLEY

(Over his shoulder) No hard feelin's. It's in the breeze. He's the one star. *(To Stan)* What's for supper anyway?

STAN

(Enthusiastically) Tuna casserole, I think.

WESLEY

That crap?

VAL

(To Randy) Did you hear me?

RANDY

Ya. *(Under his breath)* He's a f'n . . .

STAN

(To Wesley) Or maybe lasagne.

WESLEY

That'd be cool.

Just then Jim enters the corridor behind them. He sees Val and the boys.

JIM

(Calling to Val) What's up? Need help?

VAL

(Disappointed to see Jim) No. Yes. *(To the boys)* Wait here.

The boys wait while Val walks to meet Jim. They converse out of the boys' shot.

VAL

(To Jim) Can you take Wesley to Clearwater *(i.e. the isolation unit)*? Stan back to his unit? I have to talk to Randy for a minute.

JIM

What'sWhat'd Wesley do now?

VAL

(Tryingake light of it for Jim's sake) Nothing. Getting Randy riled up is all. Testingew guy. Nothing serious.

JIM

Don't it so lightly. Don't let him get away with that crap. Wesley's a manipu son-of-a-bitch.

VAL

I'll talkesley too.

The coution breaks up as they carry on with the task of managing the boys. Jim goVesley. Val stays back watching.

JIM

(To WéCom'on Chief. Need some alone time?

Jim att to grab Wesley by one arm. Wesley pulls his arm away.

WESLEY

(Angriin walk myself.

JIM

(To WéWatch yourself. (To Stan) Come'on. I'll take you back to the unit.

Jim tdesley's arm firmly and leads him to the doors at the end of the corridan follows. When they get to the doors, a brief pause, then Pshshsht. Jim anoys exit through the doors. Once they have left Val motions for Randy to follo

VAL

(To Raome'on.

They way towards Val's office.

SCENE 4 - VAL & RANDY

Val and Randy enter Val's office. There is a desk, two chairs, and Val's "evidence board" (like on the TV crime dramas) where she gathers information (newspaper clippings, articles, posters, artifacts) related to her research on youth crime. More and more items accumulate on the board as the play progresses. Once inside Val sits down at her desk. Randy stands waiting.

VAL

Well, Randy?

RANDY

Ya?

VAL

What was that? *(Motioning for Randy to sit down)* Sit.

Randy sits in a chair opposite her.

VAL

Quite a scene. I wasn't expecting that from you.

RANDY

What? He's the one . . .

VAL

You almost made me call code. That's the kind of behavior that jeopardizes our programs. Is that what you want?

RANDY

(Defensively) No. I . . .

VAL

I thought you were smarter than that. He pushed your buttons and you played right into it.

RANDY

Just wan'ed to . . . Didn' think he'd trip like that.

VAL

Wise up.

Pause.

RANDY

Am I in trouble?

VAL

I'll have to write up an incident report for your file. Wesley provoked you. You lost your temper. But fight avoided. Okay?

RANDY

I guess.

VAL

Don't let it happen again.

RANDY

Whatever.

Pause. Both are willing to settle for that outcome.

VAL

Apparently Wesley's a bit unstable.

RANDY

(Sarcastically) Oh ya?

VAL

That's what everyone says.

RANDY

What's his probl'm?

VAL

Never mind. Just watch out for him while you're here. Cut him some slack, okay?

RANDY

I guess.

VAL

Alright then.

Pause. Val gets up and begins rummaging through things on her desk.

RANDY

Your jus' new here, eh?

VAL

Yes.

RANDY

(Feeling her out) What were you doin' before?

VAL

If you want to talk, let's talk about you. Never mind me.

RANDY

(Offended) Just wonderin's all.

Pause. Val finds what she's looking for – a newspaper article. She goes to pin it on her evidence board.

VAL

(Giving in to Randy's request) I was at the University studying Criminology. Before that, mostly group homes.

RANDY

(Not ready to change the subject yet) Oh ya? Why you so interested in crim'nals?

Val sits back down.

VAL

Not that I'm so interested in criminals. I just want to help improve things.

RANDY

Like the programs?

VAL

Yes. I think the programs can make a positive difference.

Pause.

RANDY

This place only makes us better crim'nals.

Randy gets up and moves towards the evidence board to have a closer look.

VAL

That's what I mean. We should be doing more.

Pause.

RANDY

(Indicating the evidence board) What's all this?

VAL

That's stuff I've been collecting. Articles and stuff for my research.

Pause.

RANDY

(Still looking at stuff on the evidence board) Research?

Pause.

RANDY

Can I ask you somethin' 'bout my case?

VAL

I'm not sure I'm the one to talk to.

RANDY

That's the probl'm. No one'll listen. They jus' want me to answer their stupid questions.

VAL

Who does that?

RANDY

Everyone. The pigs, social workers, judge, psychologist. Even my lawyer. Just tells me what to say. No one gives a sh . . . *(Censoring himself)* crap what I think.

VAL

What is it?

Pause. Randy sits back down.

RANDY

It's wack. Never bin to jail b'fore. It's not like I'm a hard-core crim'nal. But that's how everyone's treatin' me.

VAL

It takes some getting used to.

RANDY

Don' wanna get use to it.

Pause.

ACT ONE

VAL

You should've thought of that before. We don't realize how precious our freedom is until it's taken away, eh?

Randy doesn't answer.

VAL

Look Randy, if you've broken the law, they'll find you guilty and then you might be here for a while. Best to prepare yourself for that.

RANDY

Even if they prove me guilty, don' make me guilty. Only according to their story.

VAL

There've got to be some grounds for the charges.

RANDY

My case's total bull, eh? Lawyer says not to talk 'bout it, but I gotta talk to someone.

VAL

I don't want to hear about any new crimes.

RANDY

(Jumping in) There's no crimes . . . That's jus' it. It's popo *(i.e. cops)*. *(Randy becomes more and more agitated as the speech progresses)* Got in a fight, sure. But Squirrely 'n me's always knockin' each other 'round. Ever since grade two. He was way overdue what he owed me. Knows I'll cover him in a tight spot. But he's gotta throw me some cash now 'n then, or he knows I'll come after him. Suddenly he's chargin' me for assault? Bull. I know the pigs pressed those charges.

VAL

Why would they do that?

RANDY

First I didn' know why they'd bother. Just a little fish. Then they started askin' all their damn questions. Thought I'd jus' roll over on my bros? Goofs. I didn't say a word. Which really pissed 'em off. So now they're tryin' to make those bogus charges stick?

VAL

If they haven't got a case you've got nothing to worry about.

RANDY

Meanwhile I'm stuck in here? . . . Sh . . . *(Censoring himself)* Sorry. Not sayin' I never broke any a their f'n laws. But I ain't guilty a what they're chargin' me with. It's wack man. They make rules . . . 'n then they break 'em?

VAL

You told your lawyer all this?

RANDY

I told him. But it's my word 'gainst the pigs.

VAL

Sounds like they're just trying to scare you, Randy. Squirrely would eventually have to testify. And if he won't say you assaulted him . . . ?

RANDY

Who knows what kind'a deal the cops made?

VAL

Hang in there. I'm sure the truth will out.

RANDY

Hope so.

VAL

In the meanwhile . . .

RANDY

Everyone keeps telling me: *(Mockingly)* Keep your nose clean.

ACT ONE

VAL

No point just moping.

RANDY

Easy for you to say.

Pause.

VAL

(Checking the time) Well come on, Randy. I have to get you back.

They both get up to go.

VAL

And yes . . . Watch your language in here.

Val takes Randy by the arm and leads him away. They exit.

SCENE 5 - DREAMCATCHERS

On Athabasca. Eileen is alone. There is Native powwow music playing softly in the background. Eileen spreads out a buffalo hide on the floor and sits down on it. There is a Pshshsht sound. Enter Wesley and Stan, followed by Val and then Randy. The boys go over to Eileen and stand around the buffalo hide. Wesley and Randy keep their distance from one another. Val stays in the background observing.

EILEEN

(Greeting the boys) Tân'si *(i.e. "Hello" in Cree).*

WESLEY

(Repeating "hello" in Cree) Tân'si.

EILEEN

(For Randy and Stan's sake) That's hello how are you in Cree.

STAN

(Attempting the Cree word) Tân'si.

WESLEY

What's this? *(Kicking at the buffalo hide.)*

EILEEN

That's a buffalo hide.

WESLEY

C'n see that. What we doin' with it?

EILEEN

For starters . . . I thought you might like to sit. Apih *(i.e. "sit" in Cree)*. Îkwa pîayapik *(i.e. "Come sit down" in Cree)*. Come. Sit down.

Eileen motions for the boys to sit down. Wesley sits on the hide willingly. Randy and Stan remain standing.

EILEEN

Come on. Iwî acimoyân *(i.e. "I'm gonna tell a story" in Cree)*. I have a story to tell you.

VAL

(Encouragingly) Come on guys.

Stan sits down too. Eileen and Stan shake hands.

VAL

Randy?

RANDY

No thanks.

WESLEY

(Teasing) What's a matter?

RANDY

(Sternly) Not 'n the mood.

WESLEY

Chill out dude. Last week, that was nothin'. Didn't mean nothin' by it. Just playin' ya.

RANDY

Ya, real funny. Pissed me off.

Val moves into position between them.

WESLEY

That's the point, goof.
Randy turns away from Wesley.

WESLEY

Checkin' ya out's all. Seein' what my new homey's made of.

28

RANDY

(Mumbling) Ain't your homey.

WESLEY

Y'are now, homey.

VAL

That's enough. If you want to take part in programs, you're going to have to get along. Wesley? *(Reminding him of a conversation they had earlier).*

WESLEY

I'm cool.

VAL

(Prompting him) Wesley.

WESLEY

Ya. *(To Randy)* Sor-ry Dude! Like I said. It's in the breeze. Nothin' pers'nal.

Pause. Randy pulls up a chair.

RANDY

(Looking to Val) I'll sit here, 'kay?

VAL

Okay.

Once everyone is settled, Val moves off to get the snack. Eileen holds up a beautiful, colorful dreamcatcher.

EILEEN

(With a glance in Val's direction) Look what Val brought us. Have you ever seen one of these?

The boys nod yes.

ACT ONE

WESLEY

Dreamcatcher.

EILEEN

That's right.

STAN

See'em all over. My mom had one.

EILEEN

A common spiritual item. From Ojibway culture. So let's start there today. I'm going to show you how to make them. Have you ever made one before?

The boys shake their heads no.

WESLEY

No.

RANDY

We're gonna make those?

EILEEN

Yes. But first, I want to tell you a story about the very first Dreamcatcher. Like the name says, they catch dreams. But only the bad ones. Listen. Nitohta nitacimōwin *(i.e. "Listen to my story" in Cree)* and you'll learn why. Are you ready?

A brief delay as Val passes around a snack. The boys munch their snack but are attentive. Eileen begins her story.

EILEEN

Kâyâs *(i.e. Crenglish for "a long time")* ago in the days of the ancestors, some of the children of the people were having strange and frightening dreams . . .

Fade out.

SCENE 6 - THE CRASH

Images projected on screen. This is Stan's "fantasy". (In the original production, for the video scenes, the Director had the character whose vision the video represented on stage engaged in some activity. In this case Stan was on stage break-dancing.) The images represent a comic that Stan has drawn about an escape attempt. The comic will be introduced in the following scene. We see three still images of the comic in sequence, or the images can be digitally animated with sound effects to tell the story (as was done by the Videographer in the original production).

Image 1: An overview of a parking lot. It is night. It is the parking lot of the Young Offender Centre – the same parking lot, building, fence, entranceway with sign and flag pole as in the first video "The Escape." The lights of one of the cars parked in the lot are on.

Image 2: Close up of the car – a shiny new hopped up muscle car. Through the window of the driver's seat we see a young man resembling Stan. There are two unidentifiable passengers in the car. The car is speeding past the front entrance of the building. A number of guards in uniform are running out through the doors. One of them resembles Jim who has his gun drawn and is shooting at the car.

Image 3: The car is at the end of the driveway overturned in a culvert at the side of the road with fire and explosion emanating from it. Jim is standing further up the driveway with the gun still pointed at the car. In the distance, at the entrance of the Centre others are gathered watching and screaming.

SCENE 7 - STAN'S COMIC

On Athabasca. There are a few completed dreamcatchers hanging around the space, other art materials and artworks in various stages of completion are scattered around. More and more artworks and materials accumulate in the space as the play progresses.

A Pshshsht and Randy, Wesley and Stan arrive accompanied by Val. They are just coming from school and in mid-conversation. Wesley and Randy are still keeping their distance from one another. Stan is clearly agitated.

VAL

(To Stan as they enter the unit) Relax. We'll talk to her when she gets here.

Randy begins to arrange chairs in a circle. The boys sit. Eileen arrives at the door and Val lets her in.

EILEEN

Tân'si.

STAN

(Almost accosting her) Tân'si Eileen. I have a fav'r to ask you.

EILEEN

(Sitting down) Alright.

Stan looks to Val, who remains standing, for help.

VAL

(To Eileen) I told him no, but he insisted on talking to you.

Val turns it back to Stan, who looks at her, dismayed.

STAN

You tell her.

VAL

(With a sigh) There are rumours going around that someone is planning an escape. There's going to be a lockdown and a search.

EILEEN

(Confused) What's going on?

Val looks to Stan to continue.

STAN

Think the rumours're 'bout me. But I ain't plannin' nothin'. It's this.

Stan pulls a rolled up paper from where he's been hiding it down his pant leg and hands the roll to Eileen. Eileen unrolls and studies the paper intently throughout Stan's next speech. Wesley and Randy strain for, but fail to get a closer look.

STAN

(Keeping a lookout) I'm doin' a comic. After they wouldn't let us watch Prison Break on TV on Monday . . .

WESLEY

(Indignantly) That was chapt.

STAN

(Breathlessly) It was . . . Been practicin' my drawin' in program, eh? Decided to do this comic. 'Bout a jail break. Yesterday that new kid. What's his name? From Chip? *(i.e. short for Chippewan, one of the other units.)*

WESLEY

You mean Richard?

STAN

He's watchin' me drawin' in Math. Maybe, I d'know, he said somethin' started this. Didn't even do nothin'. But if they find out, you know they'll blame me, 'n take it away *(indicating the rolled paper)*, 'n DC *(i.e. dorm confine)* me 'n doc points. Just got up to 4 *(i.e. the highest level of privilege on a point system)*. Will you take it for me Eileen? Take it away with you? Please?
Everyone looks at Eileen who chuckles and looks up from the page.

ACT ONE

EILEEN

(To Stan) You're right to come talk to me . . .

VAL

(Cutting her short) I told him if we turn them in and explain . . .

STAN

(Anxious) No. Please.

VAL

(Expecting Eileen's support) I'm sure they'll understand, right Eileen?

STAN

(Doubtfully) You think so? *(Looking to Eileen for help).*

EILEEN

Actually, Stan's probably right. If it's already caused a ruckus, they'll likely take it away and feel the need to enforce consequences.

STAN

(Discouraged) It's just a comic.

VAL

By rights I should turn these in.

EILEEN

It's not like it's a real escape plan. And he'll get punished for what? For using his imagination?

VAL

If we explain . . .

WESLEY

(Defending Stan) Come'on Val. Give'im a break. It's only a comic.

STAN

Didn't mean ta . . .

RANDY

(Also coming to Stan's defence) Just some drawings. We won't say nothin'.

EILEEN

I'll take responsibility.

VAL

Stop . . . Okay. No harm done. I guess I can let it slide. I didn't see a thing. There's no real escape plan, right?

STAN

No way.

EILEEN

Alright then. *(Eileen rolls up the paper and tucks it away)* Stan. Wah wha – tapwe kimiyosihcikan *(i.e. an expression of praise in Cree: "Oh wow, you did a good job")*. They're real careful drawings. I can see you put in lots of time and effort.

Stan, relieved, beams at the praise.

EILEEN

So why don't you tell us about your comic then. What's it about?

VAL

(Forcefully) Maybe we should drop it, Eileen.

EILEEN

Maaa *(i.e. Cree expression)*. Just a question or two. About the artwork.

Val concedes with a gesture.

STAN

Was just imaginary, you know? Like: What'd it be like to 'scape outta this place?

ACT ONE

Val laughs nervously and so does Stan. Wesley gives Stan an appreciatory slap on the back.

EILEEN

And? What was it like this escape you imagined?

STAN

(Shyly to Eileen) You saw it.

EILEEN

I did. And it didn't seem very pleasant. That's why I'm asking.

WESLEY

(Curious for more detail) What?

STAN

Was just imaginary. Just wanted to, you know, blow it up.

WESLEY

What?

RANDY

Blow what up?

STAN

(To Val) You saw it too.

RANDY

What? Just tell us.

VAL

(Matter-of-factly) The getaway car crashes and explodes.

Randy and Wesley groan in disappointment.

WESLEY

(Sarcastically) Great 'scape plan, Stan!

RANDY

Ya. That's chapt. Should least a let'em get away.

WESLEY

(To Stan) Remind me not to join your 'scape plan. *(Wesley gives Randy a slap on the back.)* Eh, Randy?

Randy eyes Wesley suspiciously, but lets it pass.

VAL

(Exasperated) There is no escape plan.

STAN

(More enthusiastically) Anyway, it's not done. Who says they don't survive. Maybe it's all part a the plan. Cause a distraction while they get away.

WESLEY

That's more like it.

The boys continue the conversation about the escape scenario and have a laugh. The atmosphere becomes more relaxed. Val goes to Eileen and says something to her privately. They have a private exchange. Then Eileen turns to the boys.

EILEEN

Ow ikosi pitamâ *(i.e. "That's it for now" in Cree)*. We better change the subject before we do get in trouble. I have a new game to show you.

Val gets the snack. She opens and hands around two bags of nacho chips. The boys begin munching. Eileen gets up and pushes her chair back. She puts the rolled paper away with her things and prepares for the game.

EILEEN

Ikwa *(i.e. "Come" in Cree)*. Let's all get on our feet in a circle. *(Eileen motions a circle with her hands.)* I brought some hacky sacs.

ACT ONE

Eileen brings out a bag of hacky sacs and tosses them one-by-one to the boys. The boys get up as they swallow mouthfuls of chips, push their chairs back, chatting amongst themselves as they get ready in a circle. They go for the hacky sacs enthusiastically and begin tossing and kicking them around.

Fade out.

SCENE 8 - JIM'S WARNING

In the corridor. Wesley and Randy are on their way to the unit – walking in the same direction, but separately, quickly, silently, heads down. Jim is passing through the corridor on his way to somewhere else. He sees Randy and Wesley ahead of him in the corridor.

JIM

(Calling out) Hey. Who's that?

Randy and Wesley turn around.

WESLEY

(Answering Jim) Wesley. And Randy.

JIM

Randy? Oh ya. Come here.

Wesley and Randy walk towards Jim as instructed.

JIM

You two decided to get along? If you know what's good for you, Randy, you'll stay away from him. Chief here is a little "erratic" *(Making crazy gestures with his hand to his head).* Found that out his first week here, right Wesley? You're not gonna try that again, are ya?

No answer.

JIM

Wesley?

WESLEY

(Disgruntled) No sir.

JIM

That's good. Glad to hear it. *(To Wesley)* Come here.

ACT ONE

Wesley takes a step closer to Jim. Randy stands watching.

JIM

You know the drill.

Wesley turns raises both his arms above his head and puts them against the wall. Jim proceeds with a pat-down. With both hands Jim pats Wesley's arms from wrists to shoulder – first one, then the other, down the sides of his torso, hips, then down each of his legs. Jim stands back and barks out his next commands.

JIM

Right foot.

Still with his hands against the wall Wesley lifts his right foot so Jim can inspect the sole of his shoe.

JIM

Left foot.

Wesley does the same with his left foot as instructed.

JIM

Turn.

Wesley complies, arms still in the air.

JIM

Okay.

Wesley lowers his arms and takes a step away from Jim.

JIM

Where are you going?

WESLEY

Athabasca.

RANDY

We were helpin' Mike with the floors.

JIM

Floor duty, eh? Both of you? I'll be checking that with Mike. *(Sending them on their way)* Hurry up then.

Randy and Wesley hurry up away. Jim stands watching after them.

JIM

No running.

Randy and Wesley slow down.

JIM

Stop.

Randy and Wesley stop.

JIM

Come.

Randy and Wesley turn and move back towards Jim.

JIM

I better not hear that you guys are in any way involved in this escape plan stuff that's going on.

Wesley smirks ever so slightly.

JIM

You think it's funny? See how funny it is after you spend a few nights in Clearwater.

WESLEY

(Covering up) No sir. Not funny at all. Just think someone's makin' up stories.

JIM

What do you know about it?

WESLEY

Don't know nothin' sir. Jus' tryin' to imagine how someone thinks they can 'scape from here.

JIM

(Forcefully) Well stop imagining.

WESLEY

Must be desp'rte . . . 'n stupid.

JIM

That's right. You're not that stupid, are you Chief?

WESLEY

No sir.

JIM

What about you Randy?

RANDY

Not me sir.

JIM

(Suspiciously) Better not find out you guys lied to me either. Now get going.

They begin to go.

JIM

Wait.

They stop.

JIM

Better not hear you saying nothing more about no escape plan. You hear me?

WESLEY & RANDY

Yes sir.

Randy and Wesley hesitate. Jim waits arms folded. Randy and Wesley turn and continue on towards Athabasca walking side-by-side.

JIM

(Calling after them) Single file. And keep your hands off the wall.

Wesley quickly steps in front of Randy and they continue walking single file heads down.

JIM

You're keeping your nose clean, right Chief?

WESLEY

(Answering over his shoulder) Yes sir.

JIM

(Threateningly) I'll see you tomorrow.

The boys continue walking.

WESLEY

(Under his breath to Randy matter-of-factly) I hate that prick.

SCENE 9 - ESCAPE PLOT INCEPTION

In Randy's room. A small "cell" with a bunk bed, two shelves, a securely encased light fixture mounted high on one wall. The light is on. It is centrally controlled and will go out partway through the scene indicating the 10:00 p.m. "lights out" for inmates. The door, which is locked, has a small window in it of reinforced glass. Beside the door, in a panel in the wall, are a button and a speaker. Randy is lying on the bottom bunk of the bed reading. We hear a Pshshsht and the door opens. Enter Wesley carrying his pillow, blanket, a few toiletries (shampoo, toothbrush, toothpaste, soap, towel, deodorant) inside his pillowcase, and a change of clothes (navy blue sweats). Randy sits up startled.

RANDY

What the fuck you doin' here?

WESLEY

Chill out. It's cool. Thought we were good.

RANDY

What the . . . ?

WESLEY

Asked Darla to change roommates. Told'er Stan's snoring's keepin' me awake. Snores like a bear. You're the only one with no roommate.

Wesley drops his blanket and pillow to the floor and starts arranging his stuff on the shelf.

WESLEY

Com'on. You're not still mad? Told you I was just trippin'.

RANDY

Don't mean I want you for a roommate.

WESLEY

Na man. Chill. Com'on. I'm the best roommate here. *(With a chuckle)* Ask Stan. I'm a chillin' person.

44

Feeling no immediate threat from Wesley, Randy resigns himself to the new arrangements and relaxes a bit.

RANDY

Whatever. Do I got a choice.

WESLEY

Not really. *(Laughs)* Hey, you know, I usually get the bottom bunk . . .

RANDY

Don't give a crap.

WESLEY

But I'm gonna let you have it. Like I said, I'm a chillin' guy.

Wesley throws his blanket, pillow and pillowcase onto the top bunk and climbs up. Randy tries to go back to his reading, but is interrupted by Wesley talking. Wesley arranges his bed as he talks.

WESLEY

So wha'da'ya think a Amy? Pretty smokin', eh? Tellin' you, she's a dime. But man, tryin' to get with 'er in here sucks. Like grade five all over. All on the down low. Sneakin' kisses, you know? It's all good though. Plan on meetin' up on the outs *(i.e. outside)*. *(Chuckling to himself)* 'Til then, do what I gotta do.

RANDY

(Mildly interested) When's she get out?

WESLEY

Got court in a few weeks. See what happens.

RANDY

An' almost a year before you're out. Think she's gonna wait for ya that long?

ACT ONE

WESLEY

Sure, she will. *(With bravado)* Promised her things she won't wanna be missin' out on. Know what I mean?

RANDY

(Sceptical) Ya sure.

WESLEY

Anyway, we both bin inside. She's cool with that. Not all girls wanna link up with a guy's bin inside.

RANDY

Ya fig're?

WESLEY

Tellin' you, Amy's choice. So gonna like gettin' with her . . . You got a honey on the outs?

RANDY

Sure, there's girls.

WESLEY

Oh ya? How many?

RANDY

A few.

WESLEY

Woo-hoo. Must be missin'em now.

RANDY

(Lightening up) Ya, sure. They're fly.

WESLEY

Word.

RANDY

But there's things I'm missin' more.

WESLEY

Like what?

RANDY

Like . . . smoke. I'm jonesin' for some bud.

WESLEY

Pash-ence *(i.e. patience)* dude. There's ways . . . Tobacco's worse. It's cold turkey in here. I was shakin' for a month. What else?

RANDY

Partyin'. Bein' able to come 'n go. Money in my pocket. Eat what I want. My clothes, man. These blues're chapt. Not use to being cooped up all day. Not sleepin' so good.

WESLEY

Only two things to do about that. There's pills. Even if the doctor won't give ya any you can always get some.

RANDY

Don't want any pills.

WESLEY

Then there's, you know, beatin' it *(Rocks the bed and makes gestures suggestive of masturbating)*. There's even guys in here'll help you with that.

RANDY

Shut up. Ain't no fag.

WESLEY

Aight. Didn't say you were. Just sayin'.

RANDY

(Annoyed) Whatever.

WESLEY

You c'n try the pills if ya want. Beds suck, food sucks, company sucks. No offence. Pills make it all better.

RANDY

(Aggravated) Will you shut up? Don't need no pills or nothin'. Just wanna get outta here.

WESLEY

It's what we all want . . . Think you're the only one's hard up?

RANDY

That's not what I meant. Just dunno how ya can laugh it off.

WESLEY

Think I'm laugin' it off, a-hole? Only way to keep from losin' it. Bin here way too long.

RANDY

Just really pissed's all. Jus' really gotta get outta here.

WESLEY

(Sullen) No kidding.

Pause.

RANDY

Didn't mean ta . . .

WESLEY

Na. You're right. *(In hushed tones)* Maybe we should go with Stan's idea. Come up with a real 'scape plan.

RANDY

Right. *(Laughing it off)* Like we're gonna get outta this place. Didn't mean 'scape. Just wish popo'd get off my case.

WESLEY

Your case? What about the rest of us? We should all 'scape together.

Randy guffaws.

WESLEY

(Hushing Randy) Why not? You heard 'bout those six guys 'scaped in Regina last summer.

RANDY

You buggin' man.

WESLEY

Think 'bout it. Why don't they want us watchin' Prison Break, huh? Why they so par'noid about rumours if it ain't poss'ble to break outta here? Hey? Tell me that?

RANDY

Even if ya could get out, think you'd get away with it?

WESLEY

Worth a shot.

RANDY

You trippin' man. Only lookin' at another year 'n you wanna run?

WESLEY

'Nother year a this? Had 'nough a this. You're the one sayin' ya gotta get out.

RANDY

But 'scapin's a wack idea. You heard Jim. He's watchin' like a . . .

ACT ONE

WESLEY

What? You 'fraid a him?

RANDY

Not afraid a him . . .

WESLEY

Nevermind. I can handle him.

RANDY

With all the rumours goin' 'round, just no point in makin' it worse.

WESLEY

Screw it. Can't get no worse. Shouldn't just take it, right? Forget Jim. Thinks he's all that. I'll show'im.

The light goes out. Their voices become more hushed. Randy places his book onto the floor under his bed and tucks in.

RANDY

(Trying to placate Wesley for the time being) Sure ya will.

WESLEY

With all the rumours it's perfect. They hear anything 'bout a plan they'll think it's just more bull. Anyway, they're not gonna hear nothin'.

RANDY

Whatever.

WESLEY

Keep it real quiet . . . Could work, don'cha think? Come'on admit it.

RANDY

Aight. Maybe.

WESLEY

Just gotta come up with a plan. Are you in?

RANDY

Ya. Ya.

WESLEY

Word. *(Excited)* And when they're not 'xpectin it, we're outta here.

RANDY

Okay.

WESLEY

They'll shit themselves. Jim'll . . .

RANDY

(Annoyed) I said okay. C'n we sleep now?

WESLEY

Aight. Sleep on it. We'll talk tomorrow.

Wesley rolls over and pulls up his blanket. Randy closes his eyes.
Fade out.

SCENE 10 - RANDY'S ROOMMATE

Randy is in the corridor with a mop and bucket mopping the floor. Val walks by on her way to her office. Randy brings the mop and follows.

RANDY

Can I talk to you for a sec?

Val gestures yes.

Once in her office Val sits in her chair at her desk. Randy leaves his mop at the door and enters, sitting in the other chair.

VAL

What is it? Heard something from your lawyer?

RANDY

(Matter-of-factly) Nothin'. Still haven't set a court date. Still investigat'n. Tryin' ta figure a way to get Squirrely to talk 'n nail me. Or some other bogus witness. Says it could be months.

VAL

They're taking their sweet time. Anyway, the time you spend here now is time served. It'll count double when you're sentenced.

RANDY

If I'm sentenced. *(Becoming agitated)* Shouldn't be gettin' any time. 'Cause I didn't . . . Didn't get caught breakin' any laws. *(Making an effort to contain his frustration)* Never thought I'd be spendin' my 18th in jail.

VAL

What? You've got an 18th birthday coming up? When is it?

Randy hesitates.

VAL

(Jokingly) Come 'on. Give it up. I can look in your file.

RANDY

Five weeks today. Hope I'm not still here. Was lookin' forward to goin' drinkin' 'n ac'chally bein' legal.

VAL

Never mind. Lots of time for drinking. I'll tell you what. If you're still here five weeks today, we'll do something special. Get a cake or something.

RANDY

(Chuckling) Ya, with a file inside.

VAL

Now, now. None of that.

RANDY

Anyway, don't wanna talk about it no more. Too depressing.

VAL

Okay . . . One day at a time, right? So . . . *(Changing the subject)* How are you getting along with your new roommate?

RANDY

Not use ta havin' a roommate. An' Wesley . . . Like you said, eh?

Pause.

VAL

(Gently coaxing) What do you mean?

RANDY

He's a bit wacked out. Buggy . . . *(More sympathetically)* Well . . . I guess, considerin' . . .

VAL

He told you his story?

53

ACT ONE

                          RANDY

Said he killed his mom.

                          VAL

He's been through a lot.

                          RANDY

Seems okay most times, but then . . . Don't think straight. Yaps on 'n on . . . And
some a the stuff!

                          VAL

Like what?

                          RANDY

Other day . . . He's on 'n on about Amy . . .

                          VAL

What about Amy?

                          RANDY

You know . . . How he's all sweet on 'er. How he's gonna get with 'er on the outs.
All mushy.

                          VAL

That's not so buggy.

                          RANDY

And about Stan's comic.

                          VAL

(More attentive) What about Stan's comic?

                          RANDY

(Finally getting to the point) The 'scape thing, you know? He's . . .

VAL

What? You said you weren't gonna talk about that.

RANDY

I know. It's what I'm sayin'. He was . . . *(Realizing he doesn't want to get Wesley in trouble)* I told him he's crazy. And to just shut up.

VAL

Well good then.

RANDY

He likes talkin' big, eh? It's just talk.

VAL

The comic was bad enough. You see what it started. Wes better cut it out.

RANDY

Maybe you can talk to 'im, eh? Don't tell 'im I said nothin' though.

VAL

I'll talk to him alright. I'm not jeopardizing programs for Wesley's big mouth.

RANDY

Don't wanna get him in any trouble.

VAL

I don't want trouble either. I'll tell him . . .

Eileen approaches Val's office door calling out.

EILEEN

Hey Val have you seen. . . *(Seeing Randy)* Here you are . . . Mike's in the hall looking for his mop.

RANDY

I better go. Thanks Val.

Randy gets up quickly takes his mop and goes.

SCENE 11 - ALTERNATIVES

Val and Eileen are alone in Val's office. Eileen has come to talk over program details with Val. Eileen wanders around the office as she talks.

VAL

The boys are really enjoying making dreamcatchers, don't you think?

EILEEN

Ya. Sure, but . . .

VAL

But what?

EILEEN

I've been thinking.

VAL

Yes?

EILEEN

Based on last week's session . . . Stan's comic, remember?

VAL

(Snapping) What about it?

EILEEN

Excuse me?

VAL

(Apologetically) I'm concerned. Apparently Wesley's been talking.

EILEEN

That's not surprising.

VAL

Exactly.

EILEEN

I mean, not surprising that the idea of an escape plan would capture their imaginations. That's my point.

VAL

Not you too?

EILEEN

A natural response to being locked up, don't you think?

VAL

Wesley's going to get us in hot water if he keeps it up.

EILEEN

That's nonsense.

VAL

You know how things go. They hear about this and programs will get shut down.

EILEEN

Just hear me out. What I'm thinking is to build on their interest. Turn it into something productive.

VAL

About the escape stuff? I don't see how anything productive can come from that.

EILEEN

It's not an escape plan. Just to focus that impulse. A catalyst for our drama.

VAL

We shouldn't be encouraging any more talk about escape. Let's just drop it.

ACT ONE

EILEEN

And miss a great opportunity?

VAL

What opportunity? To get in trouble? To get drama cancelled? You know they didn't like the idea of drama from the start.

EILEEN

(Annoyed) You hired me to facilitate programs, Val. You said you wanted to try something different. Programs that could help them think about things. Now you're telling me we can't follow through on this? What is it you want? Make up your mind.

VAL

I do want to try different things. But we can't do stuff that puts our programs at risk.

EILEEN

Change doesn't come without risk.

VAL

(Frustrated) But there's no point risking it all?

Pause. Eileen is silent.

VAL

Tell me then. What exactly do you have in mind? *(Insistent)* Nothing about escape plans or jail breaks I hope.

EILEEN

Nothing like that . . . I thought I'd get the boys improvising scenes . . . from their experiences . . . involving that impulse . . . to change things. Focus on choices, consequences, alternatives. How things could be different.

VAL

Sounds vague. How do we know . . . ?

EILEEN

It's exploratory . . . Not specifically about crime. Maybe school or family or street life.

Pause.

VAL

I guess we can give it a try. As long as we steer them away from anything too dicey.

EILEEN

I don't know what you're so afraid of. These are imaginary, like Stan says. Better to express them, than keep them in. You wanted to get them thinking. I expect the boys will come up with some pretty powerful scenarios.

VAL

That's my worry. How will staff respond if they get wind of it?

EILEEN

We'll keep it low key. I promise.

VAL

And be prepared to drop it if we need to?

EILEEN

(Vigorously) I'm not here just to keep the lid on the pot, Val. My role is to help the kids imagine life beyond this place. To figure out who they are and who they want to be . . . Dreamcatchers aren't enough.

VAL

But let's be smart about it, Eileen. We can't disrupt things too much.

EILEEN

You can't make an omelette without breaking eggs.

VAL

That's a stupid expression.

An uncomfortable silence.

VAL

Are we still going for dinner?

EILEEN

I think I'll just head home.

They get ready to go continuing talking as they exit.

VAL

Don't say anything to anyone. Let me do the explaining . . .

They exit together.

SCENE 12 - THE BETRAYAL

Video on screen. This video represents Welsey's fears. (The first production had Wesley on his bunk tossing and turning, having a nightmare.) It is shot as if from three different surveillance cameras mounted near the ceilings in three locations in the Centre: in the workshop, at the downstage end of the corridor looking upstage, and one aimed directly at the upstage set of doors. (For the first production the video director also created a shot as if from inside the air vent with the boys shown crawling through it and out a metal grate.) In the first shot we see a large room – the workshop. In dim light we see worktables and woodworking tools at one end, automotive parts in another area near an overhead vehicle door. There is welding gear in another corner. The video bears a time stamp. It reads 2 a.m. The frame is still for a while. Then we see movement near a top corner of the frame. A metal grate in the wall just below the ceiling moves. We see it being removed – a pair of hands pulls it inward into the hole in the wall behind where the grate was. Then we see a body squeeze itself through the hole, arms first, then the head, torso, etc., and drop to the floor. The body stands up. It is Wesley. All is quiet. Randy follows through the vent hole in the same way – dropping to the floor and then getting up onto his feet. Stan follows. When all three are on the floor standing up, suddenly three uniformed security staff – including Jim, arrive on scene with a crash through the workshop doors. Bright lights come on.

The boys panic for a moment, but quickly realize they are caught. Randy and Stan are grabbed, roughly by security staff, forced up against the wall, faces first and held there. Wesley who makes a move to get away is tackled to the floor by Jim. Wesley struggles, but is eventually subdued, then roughly lifted off the floor and also forced up against the wall.

JIM

(To the boys) Assume the position.

Once released all three boys stand facing the wall with legs spread and arms outstretched over their heads, hands flat on the wall. They are each patted down by a staff member. The staff person searching Randy finds a key hidden in Randy's sock. The security staff hands the key to Jim.

JIM

(With a grin) What's this?

Randy is silent.

ACT ONE

JIM

(To the boys) We'll find out soon enough. Did you really think you'd get away with this? Morons. Helping us test our security. *(To the other staff members)* Take them to Clearwater.

Each of the boys is taken roughly by a staff member. Jim grabs Wesley by the arm. They disappear out of view of the camera.
　Switch to view from a surveillance camera at the downstage end of the long corridor. The group moves up the corridor towards the set of doors at the end. Wesley is still struggling. As they near the doors the view switches.
　Switch to surveillance camera aimed directly at the doors at the upstage end of the corridor. We see the doors and through the glass we catch a glimpse of two people walking through the alcove, past the doors towards the front exit of the Centre. These people include a uniformed staff member and a young woman in civilian clothes – this is Amy, Wesley's girlfriend. We see them briefly as they pass by. On their way to Clearwater, Jim with Wesley and the other two security staff with Randy and Stan, having arrived at the doors and waiting for them to be unlocked, come into view of the camera. Wesley has noticed Amy walking by on the other side of the doors. He shouts and thrashes at the sight of her.

WESLEY

(Shouting) Amy, you didn't. Tell me you didn't.

Jim tightens his grip on Wesley.

JIM

(To Wesley) Shut up.

Wesley shouts after Amy, struggling and almost in tears.

WESLEY

Amy, how could you?

Once the alcove is clear – Amy gone, we hear the Pshshsht of the doors unlocking. The group prepares to pass through the doors. Wesley quiets down dejected.

JIM

(To Wesley, enjoying taunting him) You see Chief, true love can't compete with a promise of leniency. Learned your lesson dumbass?

The three boys are taken through the doors on their way to Clearwater. We are left with a view of the doors as they close behind them.

End of video.

SCENE 13 - AMY'S RELEASE

In Randy and Wesley's room. The light is on. Randy is lying on the top bunk reading. The bottom bunk was given over to Wesley after all. The door is propped open. Wesley enters and closes the door behind him. He paces the room frantic, distraught. Randy looks up from his book.

WESLEY

(Without looking at Randy) Amy's out. They just came to get her. I saw them go.

RANDY

(Excited) Already?

WESLEY

(Distraught) Weeks early.

RANDY

(Unsure) That's good, right?

WESLEY

Don't say that. It's not good.

RANDY

Good for her.

WESLEY

Ya . . . No. She's away from me. Didn't get to say g'bye.

RANDY

But she's out.

WESLEY

She's out! . . . I'm gonna miss her.

RANDY

Word.

WESLEY

Seein' her, everyday. Somethin' to look forward to.

RANDY

(Trying to cheer Wesley up) Why you even trippin'? Least you know she's out. Better'n in here.

WESLEY

Na. That's the probl'm. How'd I know what she's doin'? How'd I know she's not bonin' some jerk right now?

RANDY

Chill man. She's gotta do what she's . . .

WESLEY

Shut up!

RANDY

Come'on Wes. She just got out. Prob'ly on her way to the stinkin' group home. Stop thinkin' that crap. Make yourself crazy. It's not like you're married.

WESLEY

What's that mean?

RANDY

You hardly knew her. You kissed what? Three times?

WESLEY

(Kicking the bed post) Geez. The ho is out.

Pause.

WESLEY

(Changing his tactics) And that's where I'm gonna be too. She's out early means we can move ahead with the plan. Said she'd help.

RANDY

What? You told her? Thought ya said it's between us?

WESLEY

It's Amy. Need someone on the outs, eh? She can help.

RANDY

This 'scape plan . . . It's wacked. When they hear 'bout this, it'll be lockdown. Throw us in Clearwater. Is 'at what 'cha want?

WESLEY

Don't care. Whatever. Need to get outta here. *(More desperate)* And you 'n Amy's gonna help.

Randy is silent.

WESLEY

No one's gonna find out. 'Cause we're not talkin'. Amy's out. Nothin' ta worry 'bout. Just chill.

Wesley paces. Randy is silent.

WESLEY

Gotta find a way ta get a message to 'er on the sly.

The light goes out.

WESLEY

You're cool? Everythin's cool?

Wesley moves to the door and looks furtively through the glass into the unit. Then goes to his bed.

RANDY

Whatever. You're wacked. *(Mumbling to himself)* Jus' don't give 'em my name.

Pause.

WESLEY

I'll figur' it out.

Randy rolls over to go to sleep. Wesley takes off his clothes and crawls into his bed.

Fade out.

SCENE 14 - COMMODIFYING CULTURE

On Athabasca. There is powwow music playing. There are a few more dreamcatchers, as well as drawings, photos and posters on Native themes hanging on the walls. Eileen, Randy, Wesley and Stan are sitting around a big table strewn with craft materials for making dreamcatchers: 8" metal hoops, colored hide strips on spools, spools of sinew, containers of brightly colored feathers and plastic beads. Eileen and each of the boys are working diligently at making dreamcatchers and chatting lively as they work – their dreamcatchers are all at different stages of completion. The following exchange is littered with laughter and comments.

STAN

Had a dream once. Started out real good, then got nasty. Was bustin' nuts with this dime. Oh ya. Then she turns into a white snake with blue glowin' eyes 'n slithers away. I get this virus on my dick 'n go to the doctor 'xpecting him to gi'me some med'cine. 'Stead he gets knife 'n cuts it off. Swear in the mornin' it was just achin'.

WESLEY

Pro'bly 'cause you was tuggin' on it all night!

They all laugh.

RANDY

Come'on Stan. Zat a real dream or you jus' trippin'?

STAN

(Laughing) Some might'a bin real.

WESLEY

(Cutting in with a serious tone) I had a nasty dream 'bout Amy.

Pause. Now he has everyone's attention.

EILEEN

What?

WESLEY

Never mind. *(Changing the subject)* Hear what Martin said to Laura today?

RANDY

'Bout elephants gettin' herpes?

STAN

That's what Miss Colins said in science class.

WESLEY

Get out. How's a elephant get herpes?

RANDY

Think it's a differ'nt kind.

WESLEY

Remind me to wear a condom next time I go to the zoo . . .

Laughter.

EILEEN

(Jokingly) Maa *(i.e. "Oh my god" in Cree.)* I hope you weren't planning on that, Wesley.

More laughter.

STAN

I got one . . . How do you put a condom on a elephant?

A bit of commotion as everyone thinks of an answer.

WESLEY

Tell us.

STAN

Take the "f" outta "way".

ACT ONE

WESLEY

That's dumb. Ain't no "f" 'n way.

RANDY

(Laughing) That's the answer: Ain't no f'n way!

Everyone laughs except Wesley.

WESLEY

(Groans) Dumb.

EILEEN

Good one Stan. *(Referring them back to the dreamcatchers)* Have you decided on your feathers yet?

STAN

You like these colors?

EILEEN

Îhî *(i.e. "Yes" in Cree)*. Looks great. Mihkosiw ikwa askihtakosiw *(i.e. "Red and green" in Cree)*.

RANDY

I like the blue better.

EILEEN

Sîpihkosiw *(i.e. "blue" in Cree)*.

RANDY

(Attempting the Cree word) Sîpihkosiw.

They continue picking feathers. Val enters carrying a box.

RANDY

Tân'si Val.

WESLEY

Where'ya bin? What'cha got?

VAL

Tân'si. Been talking to Shelly. *(Putting the box on the table and opening it)* They asked us to make more dreamcatchers. *(Excitedly. Taking handfuls of 3" metal hoops out of the box and dropping them clankingly back in)* To send to the troops in Afghanistan.

STAN

No way. *(Excited)* They're gonna send our dreamcatchers to Afghanistan?

VAL

(Enthusiastically) Yes.

RANDY

How many they want?

VAL

Well, this box has 200.

WESLEY

200 dreamcatchers! Can we hang 'em all around before we send 'em?

RANDY

Gonna take forever.

WESLEY

Can we take pictures?

VAL

They want them for Canada Day.

STAN

Choice. Dreamcatchers for Canada Day.

ACT ONE

EILEEN

(Upset – she's been silent on the matter up until now) You've got to be kidding, Val! We're gonna spend the next two months working on these?

VAL

I told them we'd do what we can. It's the least we can do.

EILEEN

(Muttering) The least we can do.

Eileen gets up to stretch her legs and cool off. She walks around the space. Others continue making dreamcatchers and talking excitedly with Val. Wesley gets up and goes to Eileen as she's walking about.

WESLEY

Hey Eileen.

EILEEN

Yes?

WESLEY

Can you do me a fav'r?

EILEEN

Depends.

WESLEY

It's . . . If I write a letter to Amy, can you get it to her for me?

Pause.

EILEEN

You really like this girl?

WESLEY

I miss her.

EILEEN

Kîkwâya ikî powâtaman *(i.e. "What did you dream?" in Cree)*?

WESLEY

(Hesitant) In my dream . . . she was cheatin' on me.

EILEEN

(Sympathetically) Wesley. You're both so young. Don't be too hard on her.

WESLEY

I won't. I promise. Will you?

Pause.

WESLEY

Please.

Pause.

EILEEN

Our secret okay? Get me your letter and . . .

WESLEY

I got it here.

Wesley pulls a folded paper from his waistband and holds it out to her. Eileen is a little suspicious of Wesley's premeditation.

EILEEN

Okay.

She takes the letter deciding to trust him.

EILEEN

Nika wâpamâw Amy's Okâwîsisa *(i.e. "I will see Amy's Aunty" in Cree)* day after tomorrow. I'll give it to her then to give to Amy.

ACT ONE

WESLEY

Thanks Eileen.

EILEEN

Shhh. *(Concerned)* Just don't expect too much, okay?

WESLEY

No worries.

They rejoin the table to continue working on their dreamcatchers just as Val departs.

VAL

See you later.

Fade out.

SCENE 15 - RANDY'S GIFT

In the corridor. Val leaves Athabasca and heads down the corridor towards her office. Randy enters the corridor after her. Randy is carrying a small dreamcatcher behind his back.

RANDY

(Calling after her) Val.

Val stops and turns around.

RANDY

Told Eileen I needed to talk to you. She said I could.

VAL

Come'on then.

Val waits for Randy to catch up. They walk together. Randy pulls the dreamcatcher from behind his back and shyly hands it to Val.

RANDY

Made this for you.

Val takes it slightly embarrassed by her pleasure at receiving it.

VAL

Randy, you shouldn't have.

RANDY

It's okay. Lots more for the soldiers. Eileen said I could.

VAL

Thanks.

They arrive at Val's office.

ACT ONE

VAL

Come in.

Randy enters and sits. Val finds a push pin with which she pins the dreamcatcher to her evidence board.

VAL

What did you want to talk about?

RANDY

Nothin'. *(Indicating the dreamcatcher)* Just wan'ed to give ya that. So you don't have bad dreams.

VAL

(Blushing) You don't have worry about me. My dreams aren't so bad.

RANDY

No bad dreams? Lucky you . . . If they're not bad, then they must be good. What sort'a good dreams you have? Any good ones lately?

VAL

Randy. I'm not telling you my dreams.

RANDY

(Jokingly coaxing) Come'on.

VAL

No. I'm not telling.

RANDY

Come'on. Just one good one. Tell me one a yours, 'n I'll tell ya one a mine.

VAL

(Flustered) It's not that they're good even. Nothing of interest to you. Just very ordinary dreams. Nothing worth telling.

RANDY

(Feigning a bit of bravado) That's too boring. Must be 'cause your not dreamin' 'bout me!!

VAL

(Shocked at his cheekiness) What? You think dreaming of you would make my dreams less boring?

RANDY

Sure. Handsome young guy like me ta dream 'bout . . .

VAL

(Blushing more) Randy!!

RANDY

Who knows what kinda 'ventures we'd have.

VAL

(Nervously) That's enough. I don't think adventures is anything we should be thinking about.

RANDY

Come'on. Everyone needs to dream a little.

Awkward pause.

RANDY

Now I think a it. Bin a while since I had a really good dream.

VAL

I'm not going to ask what your really good dreams are about. More information than I need.

Nervous laughter from both.

ACT ONE

RANDY

(Suddenly serious) Wish I'd wake up 'n this place'd just be a bad dream.

VAL

One that the dreamcatchers missed?

RANDY

This place is like opposite a dreamcatcher. 'Stead a catching the bad dreams it steals your good ones.

Pause.

VAL

(Changing the subject) Any news about your case?

RANDY

Ya. Good news act'chally.

VAL

Tell me.

RANDY

Mom visited on the weekend, eh? Says Squirrley's mom told her Squirrley ain't gonna testify. Maybe it'll get thrown out.

VAL

That's great news. Did they say when?

RANDY

Still no date.

VAL

Can't believe it's taking so long.

RANDY

Still tryin' to pin it on me.

VAL

With any luck it'll all be over soon.

RANDY

Ya.

Val checks the clock.

VAL

Now come'on. *(Val gathers up some things and gets ready to leave)* I have a meeting. I'll walk you partway back.

Randy gets up out of the chair and approaches Val. He teasingly holds out his arm for her to take. She also jokingly slaps his arm away. They exit together.

SCENE 16 - EILEEN'S TEACHINGS

Eileen arrives at Val's office just as Val and Randy are leaving Eileen is clearly upset.

VAL

(To Eileen) Are you coming to the meeting?

EILEEN

I need to talk to you first.

VAL

Okay. I'll be right back.

Eileen continues on to Val's office. Val drops Randy off partway back to his unit and then she returns to her office. Eileen, pacing, addresses Val as soon as she steps into the room.

EILEEN

You agreed that we'd make all those dreamcatchers?

VAL

Yes?

EILEEN

Dreamcatchers for Afghanistan?

VAL

What?

EILEEN

What are you thinking?

VAL

We were making dreamcatchers. They might as well go to good use.

EILEEN

(Sarcastically) Good use?

VAL

What is this about? You said you'd . . .

EILEEN

I went along with the dreamcatchers as a way to get started with the boys.

VAL

Yes?

EILEEN

(Incensed) I wasn't expecting a production line.

VAL

Come'on.

EILEEN

Two hundred? You come'on.

VAL

(Incensed too) Forget it then. I'll tell them we can't do it.

EILEEN

Fine.

VAL

The troops won't get their dreamcatchers for Canada Day.

EILEEN

Fine.

VAL

Fine.

Pause.

VAL

It was meant as a gesture of support.

EILEEN

Support? For war in Afghanistan? I've got three cousins over there.

VAL

Exactly.

EILEEN

They shouldn't be there.

VAL

What they're doing is vital.

EILEEN

I'm not sold on the idea of war for the sake of peace.

VAL

Geez!

Pause.

EILEEN

The military . . . They take advantage of the warrior ethic . . . like they always have. They recruit Native people, our youth, to fight their wars.

VAL

Better than gangs.

EILEEN

(Cynically) Just as bad as gangs as far as I'm concerned.

VAL

What do you mean? You see the success they've had with Cadets on reserve. As a way to keep kids out of the gangs.

EILEEN

They at least give them something . . . I don't know . . . "indigenous" to identify with. Red Alert. Indian Posse. Alberta Warriors. However twisted, they involve some sort of Native pride.

VAL

Now you're supporting gangs?

EILEEN

That's not what I said . . .

VAL

Kids killing each other on the streets? *(Indicating the space around her)* You see where they end up . . . If not dead . . .

EILEEN

They both offer a sense of belonging. Appeal to the warrior ethic. But at what expense?

VAL

At least the military keeps them out of jail.

Pause. Impasse.

EILEEN

You could have consulted me.

VAL

I thought it would be good for our programs.

EILEEN

What about the boys?

VAL

What about them?

EILEEN

Do you ever think of what's best for them?

VAL

(Defensively) Of course I do. That's what the programs are all about.

EILEEN

Are you sure it's not more about . . . keeping admin happy? Being seen as successful at your job?

VAL

What's wrong with wanting to be good at my job?

Pause.

EILEEN

Anyway, it goes against protocol for us to mass produce dreamcatchers like that.

VAL

What?

EILEEN

I told you they're a spiritual item for the Ojibway people.

VAL

(Frustrated) Why didn't you say that sooner?

Pause.

VAL

(Looking at her clock) We're late.

Val leads the way out and Eileen follows.

VAL

How am I supposed to tell Shelly . . .?

They continue chatting as they head toward the doors at the end of the corridor.

SCENE 17 - PERFORMING ESCAPE

I Escaping Mall Security

On Athabasca a few days later. There are several more small dreamcatchers hanging around the space along with more drawings by the boys on Native themes. Drama program is in process. Eileen, Val and the boys are all there. The group is standing in a circle playing a ball throwing game – throwing a number of hacky sacs to each other back and forth across the circle in a pattern. This is the game Eileen taught them previously. (This game can be used throughout the play to show the progress the boys are making in working and playing together.) Energy is high. They are all laughing and interacting – dropping balls, doing tricks with them, throwing them hard or unexpectedly, or throwing several at once to surprise their partners, etc.

EILEEN

Ow ikosi pitamâ *(i.e. "That's it for now" in Cree)*. I think we're warmed up. Toss them back to me. This way.

Everyone begins tossing the hacky sacs in Eileen's direction. Eileen picks them up one by one and puts them into a bag. Wesley catches Eileen aside stooping to help her pick up hacky sacs.

WESLEY

(Privately to Eileen) Anythin' from Amy?

EILEEN

(Gently but firmly) Nothing yet Wesley. Be patient.

Wesley, clearly agitated, moves away. When Eileen has all the hacky sacs she puts the bag aside and turns back to the group.

EILEEN

Come. Grab a chair. *(Making a circle gesture with her hand)* Wâsakâmapitân *(i.e. "In a circle" in Cree)*.
The boys each grab a chair and form a circle chatting as they do. Randy grabs a chair for Eileen and places it beside her. Val stands in the background.

EILEEN

Hiy hiy *(i.e. "Thanks" in Cree)*, Randy.

They all sit still breathing heavily from the exertion – the boys wiping sweat from their brows with their T-shirts. Wesley is the last to sit. He is fidgety. Val passes around a snack of granola bars and juice.

EILEEN

We've been working on our drama skills for a few weeks now. Communicating, storytelling, improvising . . . And you see how much you've improved already.

RANDY

I guess.

Wesley and Stan also nod their heads in agreement.

EILEEN

Today, we're going to start putting them all together. I want us to pick up on . . . *(Exchanging a glance with Val)* that impulse . . . Remember? From Stan's comic . . . *(Eileen and Stan exchange a knowing glance)* The impulse that makes you want to change, to get away, to escape a situation.

WESLEY

(Challenging) What kind'a 'scape?

EILEEN

That's what I'm getting at. What kind of situations might you want to escape?

STAN

Like Prison Break.

EILEEN

(Another glance at Val) Tâpwî *(i.e. "That's right" in Cree)*. What else?

STAN

How about 'scapin' your rivals?

ACT ONE

EILEEN

What do you mean?

WESLEY

(Making a gangsta gesture with his hands) Like gangstas.

STAN

Or enemies in war . . . So they're not captured 'n get tortured 'n stuff. Like soldiers.

EILEEN

Okay.

STAN

Or like hostages.

WESLEY

Or bank robbers 'scapin' the cops.

RANDY

(Mockingly) How 'bout a guy 'scapin' his so-called boring friends?

WESLEY

Or his wife 'n kids. *(Miming taking a swig from a bottle – hoping for a laugh)* 'Scapin' into the bottle.

EILEEN

Clever Wesley.

VAL

Or a wife escaping her husband who beats her.

RANDY

Or a kid 'scapin' his parents.

STAN

Or security at the mall.

WESLEY

(In recognition) Bin there.

EILEEN

All great ideas guys. Mitonih-mîwâsin *(i.e. "Very good" in Cree)*. Wesley says "bin there" to security at the mall. Let's start with that one. Let's get up and have you show us.

Everyone pushes back their chairs and stands up.

EILEEN

Who wants to play a security guard?

Brief pause. Wesley volunteers.

WESLEY

I'll do it.

Wesley immediately takes on an authoritative stance, pulling his baggy sweatpants up high towards his chest to indicate a uniform. He's done this before – one of his schticks to make fun of authority figures. Everyone laughs.

EILEEN

Wesley, your job is to keep the mall safe and secure. Randy and Stan, you're a couple of young guys, much like yourselves, at the mall. What're you doing here?

RANDY

It's lunch 'n we're grabbin' somethin' ta eat.

EILEEN

Let's make the food court.

Eileen gestures and they move a table and chairs into place to indicate the food court. Randy and Stan sit down. Wesley remains standing in the background in his authority-figure stance.

ACT ONE

EILEEN

Are you doing anything wrong? To make security come after you?

RANDY

Don't matter if you're doin' wrong or not. He'll still come after you.

EILEEN

Tâpwî nâ *(i.e. "Is that right?" in Cree)*?

STAN

Ya! Just 'cause we look like we might get down with some thug stuff.

RANDY

They always messin' with kids at the mall.

EILEEN

Okay, I think we're on to something. Wesley, kîkwiya asci *(i.e. "Anything else?" in Cree)?*

WESLEY

Maybe security heard that somethin's goin' down. So he's on the look out. Or maybe one a these guys done somethin' before.

EILEEN

You're looking for a reason why the security guard might suspect them?

WESLEY

Ya.

STAN

Or just 'cause we're kids 'n you're a jerk.

EILEEN

Wesley, you decide about your character. Meanwhile, let's see you two *(indicating Randy and Stan)* at lunch.

Randy and Stan mime eating.

STAN

I'm havin' Chinese. BBQ ribs. *(Gesturing with his fingers)* Chopsticks.

RANDY

Mine's pizza. Pepperoni 'n sausage.

EILEEN

Ow *(i.e. "Okay" in Cree)*, Wesley.

WESLEY

(Posturing) Here I come.

Wesley walks up to Randy and Stan at the table. The improvisation begins. Everyone is in character.

WESLEY

(Angry) You kids again? What're you doin' here? You're banned from this mall.

RANDY

(Very polite) Sor-ry dude, you must be mistakin' us for someone else.

WESLEY

Don't give me that.

RANDY

We're just havin' lunch. Then goin' back to work.

WESLEY

Where do you work?

RANDY

At the carwash 'cross the street.

ACT ONE

WESLEY

Then why aren't you wearin' one a them T-shirts?

STAN

We took 'em off.

RANDY

(Nervous laugh) Don't 'xactly want everyone seein' us with those chapt shirts.

STAN

Ya, don't impress the girls.

WESLEY

Well I'm callin' over to the carwash. Check your story.

Wesley as the security guard takes a few steps away and gets on his mimed two way radio.

WESLEY

(In the background) Get me the number for the carwash 'cross the street . . . Yup . . . . yup . . .

RANDY

(Quietly to Stan) Crap.

STAN

Why'd you say the carwash?

RANDY

Couldn't think a nothin' else.

STAN

What's his probl'm?

RANDY

Remembers me from two years ago. One night with my homeys . . . Ah . . . it's a long story.

STAN

Let's bounce.

Randy nods and on a silent hand signal the two boys get up and run for it. Wesley as the security guard yells after them.

WESLEY

If I ever see you here again . . .

Fade out.

II Escaping the Gangsta

Wesley, Randy and Stan are on Athabasca. They are improvising another "escape scene" during Drama program. With each escape scene the boys gain confidence and their drama skills get progressively better. Val and Eileen are present watching on. In this scene Randy plays an older gang member. Wesley plays a youth of 15 and Stan his younger cousin, age 12. The scene is set in a deserted city alleyway. Randy and Wesley move downstage away from Stan. Stan remains standing, waiting at some distance. Wesley is receiving instructions for his first "mission" as a new gang member.

RANDY

Had to bring your little cousin?

WESLEY

It's cool. He hangs with me.

RANDY

How old's he?

ACT ONE

                              WESLEY

Twelve.

                               RANDY

Twelve?

                              WESLEY

No worries man. He's chill.

                               RANDY

He better be. Can't have you screwin' this up.

                              WESLEY

Word. You'll see.

Brief pause as Randy considers this.

                               RANDY

Better keep control.

                              WESLEY

Straight up.

Pause.

                               RANDY

Take this.

Randy hands Wesley a mimed backpack with drugs inside. Wesley takes it. Randy pulls a mimed gun from his waistband and puts it in the backpack. Wesley puts it on his back.

                               RANDY

Here.

Randy hands Wesley a mimed slip of paper with an address on it. Wesley reads it.

RANDY

Know where that is?

WESLEY

(Thinking) Sure I do.

RANDY

Do this thing 'n we're cool. Don't mess up.

WESLEY

No worries.

RANDY

Don't even think about doin' no thing or talkin' to popo.

WESLEY

No way man.

RANDY

(Threateningly) Or I'll wack your little cousin myself.

This makes Wesley fidgety.

RANDY

Go.

Wesley takes a step to go and motions to Stan.

WESLEY

(In a louder voice) Come'on.

Stan catches up to Wesley and the two boys depart together. Randy stands watching them.

Fade out.

III Escaping the Street

Wesley, Randy and Stan are on Athabasca. They are improvising another "escape scene" during Drama program. Wesley and Stan play two street youth, ages 15-17ish. The scene is set on a deserted city sidewalk bench in the very early morning hours. The boys are huddled in their jackets, coming down after a night on the streets – smoking cigarettes.

(In the first production the Director introduced, here and in the following "performing escape" scenario, the idea of Val and the boys experimenting with videotaping their improvised scenes for drama program – with the live videotaped images projected on the on-stage TV monitor. This was done to set up use of the video camera for the upcoming scene The Right Thing where the camera plays a central role. This scene began with Randy doing the videotaping. He hands the camera off to Val when he takes on the role of the police officer. Use of the video camera made some creative staging possible. The scene was set with Stan and Wesley sitting up on the backs of their chairs facing upstage away from the audience with the video camera between them and the upstage wall capturing the action (their fronts) drawing the audiences attention to the action on the TV monitor. The scene also included much playing around with the camera – e.g. When Randy first picks up the camera he plays with his fingers in front of the camera lens pretending to pinch Stan and Wesley's bums and they shoo him away. Later, as the police officer Randy points at the camera and moves toward it as if pursuing a suspect.)

STAN

Gotta get outta this city. Jona's after me again.

WESLEY

Again?

STAN

Says I still owe him.

WESLEY

Where you gonna go?

STAN

Dunno. Away from here.

WESLEY

Word.

STAN

Word.

Brief pause as they drag on their cigarettes.

WESLEY

What about home?

STAN

That's wack. Old man won't let me near the place. Tried to stab me last time.

WESLEY

Stay with one a your homeys on the rez.

STAN

Na. Can't go back there. Anyway I'm banned.

WESLEY

Drag.

STAN

Ya.
Brief pause as they smoke their cigarettes.

WESLEY

Where then?

STAN

Anywhere . . . First I gotta get me a ride.

WESLEY

What? Thinkin' ta boost some wheels?

ACT ONE

STAN

It's what I'm thinkin'.

WESLEY

Ya.

STAN

Ya.

Brief pause as they drag on their cigarettes.

WESLEY

I know a place.

STAN

Thought so.

They share a laugh, taking another drag off their cigarettes.

Just then Randy as a policeman mimes driving by in his car. The boys notice him and their demeanours change. They get ready to move, but don't run as this will attract negative attention. Randy slows down in his car and yells out to the boys.

RANDY

Get a move on. I'm by here in three minutes. If I see you in the neighbourhood I'm takin' you both in.

WESLEY

(To Stan) Come'on.

They turn to go.

Fade out.

IV Escaping Dad

Wesley, Randy and Stan are on Athabasca. They are improvising another "escape scene" during Drama program. Randy and Stan play two brothers ages 14 and 10 respectively. Wesley plays their father. The scene takes place in their home, late at night, the boys are watching TV. The father enters drunk and is abusive towards the boys. (In the first production the experimentation with the video camera continued in this scene with Val doing the videotaping.)

WESLEY

(Taking off his jacket and shoes with difficulty) Tol' ya ta be 'n bed wh'n I got home.

RANDY

You said we could watch this movie.

WESLEY

Said-no-such-thing . . . Get da HELL ta bed.

STAN

You said . . .

WESLEY

(Stern) S'd NO.

Randy motions Stan to be quiet. He turns off the TV and the light and gets up to go to bed taking Stan by one arm.

WESLEY

Wait . . .

Randy and Stan stop in their tracks. Wesley plops down onto the couch and scratches.

WESLEY

M'ke me a'san'ich firs'.

ACT ONE

Randy motions for Stan to go to bed. Stan moves to one side, but doesn't leave. Randy moves towards the mimed kitchen and feigns a look in the fridge and cupboard for some food knowing there isn't any.

WESLEY

(More to himself than anyone) Got'da muchies somethin' f'rce.

Wesley mimes turning on the TV and begins to flip channels.

RANDY

Ain't nothin' for a san'wich Dad.

WESLEY

(Angrily) Wha'd'ya a mean? Bough' groc'ies on da w'ken'.

RANDY

Been eatin' those all week Dad.

WESLEY

Y'eat ev'ythin'? L'ttle mon-grrls.

RANDY

Ain't no bread left. Or bologne.

WESLEY

W'll god dam'it, gi'me somethin'.

Wesley fights his way up off the couch, angry, and moves towards the kitchen.

RANDY

We had the last Captain Crunch for supper.

WESLEY

L'ttle mon-grrls. Eat me outa house'n home.

RANDY

There's noodles.

WESLEY

(Angrily) NOODLS.

Wesley becomes angrier and angrier as he mimes looking in the fridge and through cupboards.

RANDY

(Quietly to Stan) Go to bed.

WESLEY

L'ttle mon-grrrls . . .

Stan exits frightened. Wesley stumbles around the kitchen. Furious at finding nothing to eat, he moves in on Randy.

Fade out.

SCENE 18 - WESLEY'S MADNESS

In Randy and Wesley's room. The door is propped open. Wesley is lying curled up on the bottom bunk. Randy enters laughing to himself. He closes the door behind him.

RANDY

That's a funny movie. Chris Rock is one funny guy.

Wesley stirs and grunts.

RANDY

What'cha bitchin' about? . . . *(Teasing)* 'Cause y'ain't heard from Am-y?

Wesley doesn't respond.

RANDY

Give'er a chance.

WESLEY

(Quietly) Whatever.

RANDY

Chill. *(Not really believing this)* She'll get back to you . . .

WESLEY

(Grumbly) Missin' the point.

RANDY

What point?

WESLEY

(Getting angry) Can't do this no more. Tired a waitin'.

RANDY

(Trying to be more sympathetic) Word. But . . .

WESLEY

(Angry) Gotta get outta here.

Pause.

RANDY

(Under his breath) Just chill man.

Randy retreats to his top bunk. The rest of the scene has the boys conversing from their respective bunks.

WESLEY

Amy was suppos'ta help.

RANDY

What help? You're not still . . . *(He doesn't finish the sentence)?*

WESLEY

You said ya was in. Don't be actin' like a little girl now 'n go backin' out on me too.

RANDY

Screw that.

WESLEY

What?

RANDY

Okay.

WESLEY

What?

ACT ONE

RANDY

Okay.

WESLEY

Okay.

Randy grumbles under his breath.
Pause.

WESLEY

Gotta fig're somethin' out.

RANDY

(Trying to stall) Give it time.

WESLEY

Fuck.

Longish pause.

WESLEY

(Off on his own tangent) We use to get along, you know?

RANDY

(Lost – not sure who/what Wesley is referring to) What . . .?

Wesley is reminiscing about his mother. Randy is quiet and listens.

WESLEY

Use to go shoppin' together all the time. She'd always buy me somethin' . . . Even come ice fishin' with Dad 'n me sometimes . . . All that stopped after Dad left . . . She's bitter. Starts trippin' on me. Arguin' all the time. Over nothin' . . .

She'd get this whiney little voice drove me nuts . . . So many times I wish'd she was dead. Even told her: Wish-you-were . . .

Pause.

WESLEY

That day Sandy came by. Brought us a few beers. We're chillin' outside . . . Then Mom gets home. She's onto me right away. Never liked Sandy. Shouldn't be drinkin'. Bla, bla, bla. Remember thinkin': Shut yr hole Bitch. Wish-you-were . . . Looked down 'n there it's lying on the grass. Next thing I'm swingin' it at her. Then she's on the ground. Head bleeding . . . Sandy called the ambulance . . . But, too late . . . She's . . .

Long pause. Wesley muffles a sob.

WESLEY

(With misgivings) I think she loved me.

Fade out.

ACT TWO

SCENE 19 - THE TAKE-DOWN

Video on screen. This video represents Jim's fantasy scene. (In the original production the Director had Jim and Wesley onstage acting out the punch that Wesley threw at Jim that we hear about in the next scene. Jim deflected the punch, wrestled Wesley to the ground, wrenched his arm behind his back and then took him away.) This video is shot as if for a reality cop show; live on-the-scene, complete with voiceover giving play-by-play details. The camera is hand-held so shaky throughout. The video switches between medium/long shots and close ups. The atmosphere is tense and chaotic as the camera crew descends upon the scene of a crime in progress. The video begins with camera adjustments.

VOICE OF COMMENTATOR

Ready?

Shot of the front entrance of the Young Offender Centre including the flagpole with flapping Canadian flag.

VOICE OF COMMENTATOR

We're here tonight with The Scene of the Crime witnessing a jail break in progress. Something I bet you thought you'd never see.

Sound of a screeching car. Camera pans to long shot of a car at the far end of the parking lot speeding out of its stall.

Close up on faces of two concerned women: Val and Eileen.

VAL

Oh no.

Pull back to show them handcuffed and in the custody of two police officers (In the original production the Video Director had the police officers in red Mountie uniforms). Jim, along with other police officers, stands watching.

VOICE OF COMMENTATOR

This quiet provincial youth detention facility is the scene of tonight's action.

Long shot as the car approaches the front entrance. Jim rushes out to the driveway, standing in the way of the car, pointing his gun.

VOICE OF COMMENTATOR

Officer Jim Hickok is on the job.

Shot of the car approaching. Switch to shot of Jim standing ready. Back to a closer shot of car approaching. Back to a shot of Jim standing ready.

Close up of Wesley's face in the driver's seat window.

Close up of Jim firing his gun. Sound of shots hitting the windshield and the car screeching to a halt.

Shot of the car. Windshield shattered, stopped in the middle of the driveway. Jim arriving at the diver's side, opening the door and hauling Wesley out of the driver's seat. We hear grunts and groans. A shot of Jim throwing Wesley against the car.

JIM

Hands on the hood. Spread your legs. *(Louder)* I said spread 'em.

Wesley complies. Jim frisks him briskly.

JIM

Hands behind your back. One at a time.

Wesley complies. Jim handcuffs him and drags him by the arm to the front door of the centre, past the cameras and Val and Eileen watching.

Close up of Wesley's face almost in tears.

Close up of Jim's face smiling proudly. He glares at Val & Eileen as he passes.

JIM

(To the camera) We got 'em.

Close up of the faces of Val and Eileen looking concerned.

VAL

Wesley.

Pan back to the car where another officer is handcuffing Stan and Randy.

ACT TWO

VOICE OF COMMENTATOR

There you have it folks a foiled jail break thanks to the efforts of Officer Jim Hickock and his crew. How about that? Live action footage on The Scene of the Crime.

Pause.

VOICE OF COMMENTATOR

That's it.

Final long shot of all the uniformed officers and their prisoners retreating into the building.

VOICE OF COMMENTATOR

That would have been more exciting if they'd actually got away. Car chase maybe?

End of video.

SCENE 20 - VAL'S CUT

In Val's office. Val is working on her "research/evidence board". The board is, at this stage, a messy collage of photos, newspaper articles, posters, and other artifacts related to Val's research on the topic of youth crime and youth justice. There's a new poster on the board which says: "If you have come to help me you are wasting your time. But if you have come because your liberation is bound up with mine, then let us work together." An image of the poster appears on screen.

Val is arranging and re-arranging the pieces anxiously. She is drinking coffee, pacing and jittery, biting her nails. She takes a few steps back, staring at the board thinking, biting her nails. After a moment of this she tears a piece of her fingernail away with her teeth and along with it a piece of skin. Her finger bleeds. She plunges it into her mouth. She's agitated and near tears.

VAL

(Finger in and out of her mouth) Ouch . . .!

Val grabs a tissue from a box on her desk, wraps it tightly around her wounded finger and holds it. She searches through her drawer, finds what she's looking for – nail clippers. She sits down in her chair, and begins examining her bleeding finger under the tissue wrap. Using the nail clippers she attempts to doctor the ragged nail. This continues throughout the exchange that follows. Enter Eileen quietly. Val notices her.

VAL

Eileen. *(Indicating her wounded finger)* Hangnail.

EILEEN

I spoke with Wesley. He's fine. Just his shoulder.

VAL

They told me. Kept him in the infirmary overnight. They let you see him?

EILEEN

He asked to see me.

Val nods in approval, but is clearly dismayed.

ACT TWO

EILEEN

Says he didn't even get a good punch in. Jim over-reacted.

VAL

(Exasperated) Wesley.

EILEEN

Are you okay?

VAL

Won't stop bleeding.

EILEEN

Let me see.

Val holds out her finger. Eileen inspects it.

EILEEN

(Indicating the drawer) I know you've got a band-aid in there somewhere.

Val nods yes still holding her finger. Eileen goes through the desk drawer, finds the band-aid box, takes out a band-aid, hands it to Val, puts the box on the desk. Val puts the nail clippers and bloody tissue on the desk and begins applying the band-aid. Before sitting back down Eileen takes Val's bloody tissue and pins it to the evidence board. Val fights back a sob.

EILEEN

What is it?

VAL

(Frustrated) It's just . . . What does Jim expect with his stupid comments all the time? He knows Wesley isn't stable.

EILEEN

Jim thinks he's being funny.

VAL

I could slug him myself sometimes.

EILEEN

Me too.

VAL

And Wesley knows better. I thought we were getting somewhere with him.

EILEEN

We are.

VAL

Meanwhile Wes's back in solitary. And Jim's fuming. Saying our programs are to blame . . . That they're destabilizing things.

Val looks at her bandaged finger and fights back another sob.

VAL

Just when I think we're making progress . . .

Pause.

VAL

I thought, while we had them here, safely locked up, maybe we could accomplish something.

EILEEN

Wesley's acting out doesn't mean we're not accomplishing anything.

VAL

It's obviously not enough.

EILEEN

You can't expect change overnight.
Pause.

ACT TWO

VAL

What you said before. That I'm more concerned about my job than the boys. You think that's true?

EILEEN

I can't tell you what's in your heart.

Pause.

VAL

(Not the answer she hoped for) Do you think our programs are useless? Or destabilizing like Jim says?

EILEEN

(Off-handedly) If they're destabilizing Jim's world, that's a good thing!

VAL

Seriously.

EILEEN

The programs are great Val. Like you want . . . They are making a difference . . . Giving the kids something productive to do, a chance to express themselves, to be creative, learn new skills . . . And getting them to think too . . . About how their lives could be different . . . Still . . . It's got to be more than that.

VAL

What more?

EILEEN

For me it's . . . about the boys. What do they need that I can give them? How can I show them that I care? It's about the relationships I build with them.

VAL

(Tritely) Relationships?

EILEEN

I mean connecting with them on an emotional level. One human to another. Even with all our flaws and weaknesses showing.

VAL

Sounds messy.

EILEEN

That's how it is. What we're into here is messy stuff.

Pause.

VAL

I suppose.

Pause. Val gets out of her chair drawn back to the evidence board, back to rearranging things, now more calmly and focused.

VAL

(Mumbling) I don't know . . . Maybe if we . . .

Eileen gets up.

EILEEN

(Casually) Don't forget to put away the nail clippers.

Focused on the evidence board Val doesn't notice as Eileen quietly slips out. Turning around Val notices Eileen is gone. She picks up the box of band-aids from the desk where Eileen has left it.

Fade out.

SCENE 21 - RANDY'S BIRTHDAY

Val's office. Val is alone. It's lunch time. Randy arrives having been instructed to stop at Val's office during the lunch break. Val is pretending to be angry. Randy is sullen.

RANDY

You wanted to see me?

VAL

(Indicating the chair) Sit.

Randy sits. Val pulls out a box from under her desk and places it in front of Randy.

RANDY

(Curious and a bit concerned. Randy thinks he's in trouble) What's this?

VAL

You'll see.

Randy opens the box hesitantly and then brightens up when he sees a McDonald's bag inside.

RANDY

Ah!

VAL

Surprise. Happy Birthday!!

She sings a few bars of Happy Birthday to him.

RANDY

(Clearly cheered up and a little embarrassed) Didn't think you'd remember.

Randy opens the bag and digs into the food beginning with fries and then a burger.

VAL

I told you we'd do something special. And I have a cake for later. DQ Chocolate Extreme Blizzard!

RANDY

(Impressed) Cool.

VAL

The guys said it's your favourite.

Pause while Randy is eating.

VAL

So how does it feel to be 18?

RANDY

(Between bites) Pretty much the same. Want a fry?

VAL

No thanks. You go ahead.

RANDY

Thanks for gettin' me some.

VAL

You're welcome.

RANDY

Can't count how many a these I eaten in my life.

As Randy continues eating he reminisces – with a bit of pride, but even more amazement at his own past experiences.

ACT TWO

RANDY

When I's 12 . . . My little brother 8 'n my sister 14 . . . Mom used to take off with her boyfriend, eh? . . . They'd be gone days sometimes . . . No grub in the house . . . Sister would cry her eyes out. . . We used ta dream 'bout cheese burgers . . .

Sometimes I'd take my little brother to the supermarket . . . We'd get a cart 'n go up 'n down the isles fillin' it up with all the stuff we liked . . . Just like we're suppos' ta be there . . . No one ever noticed us . . . Figured mom's around somewhere . . . When we got all we wan'ed . . . Pushed the cart out the door . . . And soon as we're 'round the corner we'd run like hell all the way home . . . *(Laughing)* We'd have all the grub we wanted for a few days . . . Did that so many times 'n never got caught . . . That was six years ago. . . Since then I bin inta every kinda crap you c'n 'magine.

VAL

You did what you had to do survive, Randy.

RANDY

Use ta think I'd never make it to 25.

VAL

And now? What do you think now?

RANDY

Don' know. Guess I'd like to.

Pause.

VAL

You said before that this place steals your dreams. Don't let it Randy. They can lock you up, right? But they can't take away your dreams. Don't give up on those. You have a lot to look forward to. You're smart. You can be whatever you want to be.

RANDY

Maybe.

Finishing up his food.

VAL

(Standing up and reaching out her arms) Com'ere. Let me give you a birthday hug.

Surprised Randy stands up wiping his hands and mouth on his serviette. Val nudges towards him and he leans towards her. They hug an awkward little hug. Then Randy retrieves his food bag.

VAL

Are you done? I'll take you back to school.

RANDY

(Reaching into the bag and pulling out an apple pie) Can I take this with?

VAL

Sure. But don't eat it in class.

RANDY

'Kay.

Randy tucks the pie into his sleeve. They exit together.

SCENE 22 - JIM'S REPRIMAND

In the corridor a couple of days later. Val is walking one way down the corridor and Jim is walking in the opposite direction. Val nods to Jim as she passes him. Jim turns back towards her.

JIM

Val.

Val turns around.

VAL

Ya?

JIM

How's Randy?

VAL

He's fine. Still no court date.

JIM

I heard you had a fancy cake for his birthday the other day.

VAL

And?

JIM

Do you think that's appropriate?

VAL

Think what's appropriate?

JIM

A cake?

VAL

It was his 18th.

JIM

And what? You wanted him to feel good about that?

VAL

Yes. Why not?

JIM

He's in jail for a reason.

VAL

He deserves to celebrate his birthday.

JIM

Says who?

VAL

Look. If you don't want to get him a cake, fine. I'll get him a cake if I want to. Leave it alone.

JIM

It's not my job to leave it alone.

VAL

Whatever. It was just a cake.

JIM

He'll get the wrong idea.

VAL

What wrong idea? That I care?

JIM

Don't play dumb. You coddle these kids and they take advantage. You see what happened with Wesley.

VAL

What does that have to do with anything?

JIM

You're showing them the wrong kind of attention. They need structure and discipline. Not your affection.

VAL

You do it your way and I'll do it mine. Okay?

JIM

Not okay if I'm the one taking the punches.

VAL

(Angry now) Wesley didn't even land a punch. Anyway, you bring it on yourself.

JIM

(Shocked) What'd you say? What kinda bitch remark is that?

VAL

What'd you call me?

JIM

I don't have to put up with that . . .

VAL

And I don't have to put up with your . . . *(Stopping herself)* Never mind.

She turns to go.

JIM

I'm keeping an eye on you.

VAL

Whatever.

She continues walking. Jim stands watching her until she's out of site. Then he turns and walks away in the other direction.

Fade out.

SCENE 23 - THE REJECTION

Video on screen. This video represents Randy's fear. This video is shot in melodramatic silent movie style in black and white with background music and text captions. The setting and costumes are the same as for the rest of the play. (In the first production Randy was on stage in his bunk dreaming.)

In Val's office. Randy is sitting in a chair crouched over with his head in his hands. He is sobbing heavily. Val is standing over him looking angelic with her hand on his back, giving him comfort.

Caption: Randy what ever is the matter?

Randy gets up suddenly and starts walking around the space frantic, flailing his arms. Val stands by dumbstruck listening intently to his rant.

Caption: It's my friend Wesley. He's gone mad. We have to help him.

Val follows Randy around the room trying to get him to calm down.

Caption: What can I do to help?

Randy stops suddenly. He places his hands on Val's shoulders and gazes into her eyes.

Caption: You'd better sit down.

Val pulls up a chair and sits. Randy continues to pace, but more calmly now. Trying to remain as calm as possible he explains to her in much detail what he needs.

Caption: We're planning an escape. We need your car.

Val stands up suddenly distraught, hands to her head in despair, almost hysterical.

Caption: Don't make me choose between you and the Law.

Randy takes Val by the shoulders and gives her a good shake to calm her down. They stare into each others eyes. Then Randy bends down on one knee holding her hand.

Caption: You know how much I care for you Val.

Val slaps Randy hard across the face. There is a moment where both parties stand looking at each other stunned.

Caption: I can't.

Val turns away from Randy holding the back of one hand to her forehead in damsel in distress fashion. Randy grabs onto her other arm as Val tries to get away.

Caption: Never.

The struggle continues. Randy still holding onto her one arm pleads with her. Val continues to try to get away.

Caption: Code 44 – Staff member in distress.

End of video.

SCENE 24 - GET-AWAY CAR

In Randy and Wesley's room. The door is propped open. Randy is lying on his top bunk reading. Wesley enters excitedly and closes the door behind him. He immediately pulls a folded piece of paper from his waistband. The entire conversation is in hushed tones. Wesley paces.

WESLEY

(Quietly, struggling to contain his excitement) I got it. *(Showing Randy the paper)* Message from Amy. We're good to go.

RANDY

She's actually gonna . . .?

WESLEY

Course. Think she wouldn't? Meetin' us at the fence. It's all worked out.

RANDY

First you gotta get to the fence.

WESLEY

All worked out too.

RANDY

What? You got a plan? To get outta the building?

WESLEY

Told you.

RANDY

(Still sceptical) Let's hear it.

WESLEY

Stan's idea . . .

RANDY

(Annoyed) What? Stan too?

WESLEY

Ya Stan. You 'n me 'n Stan. Not like you're much help.

Silence from Randy.

WESLEY

He fig'red a way out. His idea in the first place.

RANDY

So?

WESLEY

What?

RANDY

(Angry) What's the plan?

WESLEY

(More hushed) Air vent.

RANDY

Air vent?

WESLEY

(Shh's Randy) Shhh. It c'n work. *(He moves closer to Randy and whispers)* The air vent by the door. Be a tight squeeze. Crawl over to the shop. Kick through the door. Ain't no-thing.

RANDY

(Sarcastically) Ain't no-thing? Really think you c'n get away with it?

WESLEY

Better'n just sittin' here.

RANDY

(Sitting up on the edge of the bed) No. Think about it. You got another year. I could get out anytime. Stan'll be back'n a few weeks anyway. What's the point?

WESLEY

Easy for you to say. Whole year. And two years probation. It's a joke. Forget that. Gotta see Amy.

RANDY

When's it goin' down?

WESLEY

That's for me ta know. I'll tell ya when it's time.

Pause.

WESLEY

You down?

RANDY

It's bull.

WESLEY

Ya? Amy's helpin' from the outs. Stan's big idea. Now alls we need's a ride ta get away. That's where you come in homey.

RANDY

(Getting down off the bed) What? Me? Stan can hot wire somethin'.

WESLEY

If we hav'ta. Rather have a sure thing. Ride with a key.

Now Randy paces nervously while Wesley is calm and deliberate.

RANDY

I'm suppos' ta get that? You're nuts.

WESLEY

You good with Val, eh?

RANDY

What? You're talkin' about Val's car?

WESLEY

Val's car! It'll be your con-tri-bu-tion.

RANDY

How?

WESLEY

Go talk to 'er in 'er office. Like ya always do. And lift her key. It's no-thing. Time she fig'res it out, too late. Car's here overnight. And we're out.

RANDY

That's wacked. I'm just suppos' ta take her car key? Think it's that simple?

WESLEY

Don't matter. Your big brain'll figure it out. Long as we're outta here.

Randy grumbles under his breath.

WESLEY

Gotta sweet talk her bro. Make her trust you.

RANDY

That's crap man.

Pause.

ACT TWO

WESLEY

Either you get the key, or I'll . . .

RANDY

What?

WESLEY

Don't wanna hav' ta hurt 'er Randy.

RANDY

You . . .

WESLEY

(In a very serious tone – threatening Randy) Sorry man. But you know how it is.

RANDY

(Turning away) You're a real jerk. Know that?

WESLEY

Ya, well . . . Either ya get the key . . . Or maybe she'll give it to ya. *(Laughing)* Val can be our inside man. She likes you Randy. Thinkin' she might just go for it.

Pause.

WESLEY

Now you down or what?

RANDY

(Getting back up onto the top bunk) Aight. Aight. Don't go trippin' man. Don't do nothin'. I'll get the f'n key.

WESLEY

You better.

RANDY

(Quietly) Can't believe it . . . *(grumbling under his breath).*

WESLEY

Shhh. Aight. That's better. You'll see. It'll all work out. We're gettin' outta here . . . Now . . .

Wesley goes to the door, pushes the button and stands looking out the window waiting for attention.

WESLEY

I gotta drop a duce.

We here the Pshshsht sound of the door unlocking. Wesley exits the room. Randy is distraught. He lays his head down and closes his eyes.

Fade out.

SCENE 25 - RANDY'S DREAM

Randy is alone in the cell that he shares with Wesley. Randy is lying on his bed with his eyes closed. Enter Eileen through the closed door. Slowly a mist begins to fill the room and the sound of Native flute music is heard – giving the scene a dreamlike quality. (In the first production the Director staged this scene with Eileen standing centre stage and the actress playing Val crouched in front of her videotaping Eileen close up. Eileen's image from the camera was projected on the TV monitor. The actor playing Jim stood at the TV monitor with a wireless camera picking up the image on the TV monitor, transmitting it to the projector in the control booth, which then projected the image onto the large screen. The feedback loop produced from this set up created an image with a grainy, flickering quality that worked wonderfully as a dream sequence. The transformation of Eileen into the Bear towards the end of the scene occurred by focusing the camera on a youth's drawing of a bear that Eileen held up. The projected medicine wheel was also a drawing held by Eileen as well as a close up on her earring in the form of a small medicine wheel.) When Randy opens his eyes after a few seconds he sees Eileen there. He quickly gets up into a sitting position on the edge of his bed.

RANDY

(Surprised to see her) Eileen! What're you doin' here? It's late.

EILEEN

Îhîtâpwî *(i.e. "Yes, it's true" in Cree).* I brought you these to finish your drawing.

Eileen holds out a small bundle of colored markers – yellow, red, blue. Randy reaches out and takes them from her.

RANDY

Thanks. Just doin' the finishin' touches.

Randy pulls a large sketchbook out from under his blanket. He opens the sketchbook. Projected on screen is an intricate pencil drawing on a Native theme – e.g.) a buffalo skull with horns and feathers – a medicine wheel at its forehead.

EILEEN

It's a good drawing, Randy. Mitonih-kimîyosîhcikân *(i.e. "You did a really good job" in Cree).* Symbolic. Kohkum *(i.e. "Your Grandmother" in Cree)* will like it. She'll hang it for everyone to see.

RANDY

Hope so. Thanks for the markers. Now I c'n finish colorin' the med'cine wheel.

Randy begins coloring part of the drawing.

EILEEN

You and Wesley are up to something. You seem upset.

RANDY

It's Wesley. He's got crazy ideas.

EILEEN

Ka *(i.e. "Oh?" in Cree)*?

RANDY

Amy's messin' him up.

EILEEN

Îkwa kîya *(i.e. "And you?" in Cree)*?

RANDY

I'm fine.

EILEEN

I don't think so.

RANDY

I c'n deal.

EILEEN

You could talk to someone. You can talk to me. Or Val. She trusts you, you know? Pokowanima tatâpwakîyihtaman *(i.e. "You must trust" in Cree)*. Trust is key.

RANDY

Ya?

ACT TWO

EILEEN

I know you don't want to disappoint her.

RANDY

I don't. But, either Val or Wesley's gonna be disappointed.

Randy puts the sketchbook and markers down on the bed beside him. He lies back and closes his eyes.

RANDY

What should I do?

Through costume, lighting and images on screen Eileen transforms into a Bear.

EILEEN

(As the Bear) The medicine wheel in your drawing . . . You're its centre.

RANDY

(Sleepily) I am?

EILEEN

(As the Bear) Kawîcîhikon *(i.e. "It will guide you" in Cree).*

Eileen exits quietly along with the mist and the flute music. Randy is alone in his bunk, eyes closed.

Fade out.

SCENE 26 - BUILDING TRUST

In Val's office. Val is fiddling with the "evidence board." Randy looks on.

VAL

So? What's up?

RANDY

It's Wesley, eh?

VAL

(Distractedly) Yes?

RANDY

I dunno . . . He's wacked.

VAL

What now?

RANDY

Bein' crazy's all.

VAL

Crazy how? Crazier than usual?

RANDY

Ya. You know. He's all chill on the outside. Like ain't no-thing. But I think he's real messed up inside.

Val gives Randy her attention.

VAL

What makes you say that?

ACT TWO

RANDY

Other day before bed he's just . . . really bummed. Talkin' about his mom. Think he's feelin' it more'n he lets on.

VAL

You think he needs more help? Maybe he should go for another stint at Alberta Hospital *(i.e. A psychiatric hospital).*

RANDY

Not there. Says the place sucks. Worse'n here.

VAL

Is that right?

RANDY

Says the kids're weird, 'n the doctors're creepy. Just give ya pills.

VAL

If not there then what?

RANDY

Somethin' to help 'im . . . get over it. Just really messed up, you know?

VAL

(Agreeing) With good reason.

RANDY

Ya, but he's gotta deal.

VAL

I'll mention it to Leslie. Maybe she has some ideas.

RANDY

Not her. Psychologists are useless. What about Eileen? Maybe she c'n talk to 'im.

134

VAL

She talks to him all the time.

RANDY

(An idea suddenly comes to him) Or maybe we c'n do a sweat for Wesley. Maybe that'll help 'im. Do ya think?

VAL

That's a great idea Randy. Give us a reason to finish our sweat lodge. I'll talk with Eileen.

Pause.

VAL

Good of you to look out for Wesley like this.

RANDY

What're roommates for . . . *(Trying to sound nonchalant)* You know, he's got all these big plans to meet up with Amy, eh? And still talkin' about escapin'.

VAL

What? I thought we put an end to that. What's he saying?

RANDY

(Covering up the whole truth) How he's gotta find a way outta here. Desperate to be with Amy. How he'll do anything.

VAL

No wonder he's got you worried.

RANDY

Just real depressed, ya know?

VAL

It's bound to lead to no good.

ACT TWO

RANDY

Get 'im in more trouble. That's what I's tellin' him.

Pause.

VAL

You're right, Randy. We have to do something for him.

Val turns her attention back to the "evidence board." Randy stands up and moves towards the "board" following her. He inserts himself in the little space directly between Val and the "board." They are very close. Val takes half a step back.

VAL

(Taken aback) Randy. What is it?

Randy takes Val by one hand. Val allows it.

RANDY

(Looking down at Val's hand in his, in a very serious tone) Thanks for helpin' Wesley . . . It's serious . . . *(Looking into her eyes)* We need to do the sweat soon.

Val raises her other hand to Randy's.

VAL

I said yes, Randy. Don't worry.

Val starts to pull her hand away, but Randy holds on.

VAL

I'll talk to Eileen right away.

RANDY

Thanks.

Enter Eileen who sees Val and Randy in the hand holding position.

EILEEN

(Surprised) Oh!

136

Val and Randy drop hands simultaneously. Randy goes back and sits down sheepishly. Val, a little flustered, goes back to her evidence board.

VAL

We were just talking about you.

EILEEN

Oh?

RANDY

(Shyly) Tân'si.

VAL

Randy is worried about Wesley. *(To Randy)* Why don't you ask her?

RANDY

Wesley's actin' crazy again. I's hopin' we c'n do a sweat for 'im.

EILEEN

(Pleasantly surprised at Randy's insight) Randy. That's a wonderful idea.

VAL

That's what I said.

EILEEN

(With certainty) It'll do him good.

RANDY

(Pleading) C'n we do it soon? Please?

EILEEN

We've been neglectful about finishing the lodge, haven't we? Let's try for this weekend. If there's nothing else planned . . . I'll arrange for an Elder. Maybe Steven's available.

ACT TWO

RANDY

D'you think so?

EILEEN

Yes, you're right Randy. This is exactly what Wes needs. The healing power of the sweat will help him reconnect with his spirit. Best thing for him.

RANDY

Hope so. For Wes's sake. *(Consulting Val's clock)* Val . . . I gotta get back.

VAL

Right *(She gets ready to go)*.

EILEEN

(To Val) Do you want me to take him?

VAL

Would you please?

EILEEN

Come'on Randy.

Randy gets up. Together Randy and Eileen move toward the door making plans for the sweat.

EILEEN

Can you help me tomorrow afternoon with the willows? *(To Val over her shoulder)* I'll be right back.

RANDY

(Over his shoulder) Thanks Val.

Eileen and Randy exit still chatting. Val is alone in her office. She takes a breath. She sits down slowly in her chair, places her hands in her lap and stares at them thinking.

Fade out.

SCENE 27 - DENIAL

Vals' office a few moments later. Val is still sitting in her chair thinking. Eileen re-enters.

VAL

(Caught off guard) You're back.

Eileen sits down in the chair opposite Val's desk.

EILEEN

(Smirking) So what was that?

VAL

(In denial) What?

EILEEN

With Randy?

VAL

(Panicky) That? . . . He's worried about Wesley.

EILEEN

That's it?

VAL

I think so. *(Evasive)* Why do you ask?

EILEEN

Just seems like there's more to it?

VAL

What?

139

ACT TWO

EILEEN

I wondered if you knew anything.

VAL

He hasn't said anything to me. No news about his court case. He's being very patient.

EILEEN

That's not what I'm talking about.

VAL

What then? He's a good kid. He's got his head together. He'll be fine.

EILEEN

(Blurting it out) Val, I think he likes you.

VAL

Of course he likes me. At least I hope so. And I like him. We've bonded.

EILEEN

I mean more than that.

VAL

What are you talking about?

EILEEN

I mean . . . I think he's interested in you.

VAL

(Self-consciously) Get out. Don't be ridiculous.

EILEEN

(Teasing) I think he's sweet on you, Val.

VAL

(Blushing) It's nothing like that. I'd never encourage that.

EILEEN

Didn't say you're encouraging it.

VAL

I'm telling you . . . It's nothing to worry about.

EILEEN

I'm not worried.

VAL

Well good then. You're the one who said relationships are important.

EILEEN

(With a chuckle) I think it's cute.

VAL

Cute? Eileen. Don't say that?

EILEEN

(Laughing – enjoying seeing Val squirm) Whatever you do, don't break his heart.

VAL

Stop that. It is not funny.

EILEEN

It's okay . . . *(More seriously)* It happens. No big deal. But don't take advantage either.

VAL

What are you talking about?

ACT TWO

EILEEN

I mean . . . You can have a positive influence on him.

VAL

I think I already do.

EILEEN

Well, this is part of it. There are big feelings involved when people care about each other.

Pause.

VAL

(Flustered) Why do I feel caught out when I haven't done anything.

EILEEN

Sure you're not a little sweet on him too?

VAL

Eileen. What are you saying? Stop that. I would never . . .

EILEEN

Oh believe me . . . *(Feigning heat)* I notice those strappin' young bodies too.

VAL

(Scandalized) You don't . . . How could you?

EILEEN

What? I can't have lusty thoughts now and then?

VAL

Really . . . The boys?

EILEEN

(Still teasing) Don't look at me. You're the one holding hands.

VAL

(Looking around anxiously) Shhh! Don't say that.

EILEEN

(Playing – ominously) Oh, that's right. The walls have ears.

VAL

(Trying to avoid the subject) It was . . . He was worried about Wesley is all.

EILEEN

Sure he was.

VAL

(Looking for an escape from Eileen's teasing) I need a coffee. Go get me a coffee.

Eileen continues in the teasing tone.

VAL

Go.

Val shoos Eileen away. Eileen exits laughing.

SCENE 28 - THE SCANDAL

Video on screen. This video represents Val's unconscious fantasy. This video is shot in a wannabe Hollywood romantic feature film style, with soft edges contrasted with the harsh reality of the Edmonton landscape. Romantic music is playing. (In the first production Val remained on stage day dreaming.)

The camera is focused on the diver's side of a car. Val is sitting in the driver's seat mock Hollywood starlet style – a close-up on Val's face. Val's head is turned in the direction of the camera. She looks momentarily anxious. Then a huge smile breaks out across her face. We see Randy appear on screen from the direction in which Val was looking. He is still wearing his jailhouse navy blue sweats. He runs around to the passenger's side of the car. Val follows him with her glance. He gets into the car in mock romantic hero style. They gaze into each other's eyes for a moment. Then Val starts the car and pulls away. The camera stays focused on the car as it disappears down a quiet country road into the distant Alberta landscape. (In the first production the video director partly animated this video to have a radiant yellow glow around the characters. In the final shot the car is animated as it disappears down the road and animated flowers pop up along the roadside.)

End of video.

SCENE 29 - JIM'S ACCUSATION

Val and Eileen are walking down the corridor together chatting. Jim enters the corridor through the glass doors at the far end. He walks quickly to catch up with Val and Eileen calling after them – rudely.

                              JIM

Hey.

Val and Eileen notice him following, but continue walking and chatting. Jim catches up with them. He begins talking immediately with no attempt at civility – primarily addressing Val. He holds up a folded piece of paper – the letter from Amy, which Wesley had earlier.

                              JIM

Do you want to tell me what Wesley is doing with a letter from Amy?

Eileen immediately shrinks into the background, quiet.

                              VAL

What are you talking about?

                              JIM

I just found Wesley with it. Obviously she's responding to a letter from him. Listen: *(Reading from the letter)* Dear Wesley. I miss you too. And yes, I still want all our plans to come true. I'll do anything, bla, bla, bla.

                              VAL

Why are you asking me?

                              JIM

They're exchanging letters!

                              VAL

And?

ACT TWO

                                JIM

And someone must be helping them.

                                VAL

Well . . . *(Trying to be helpful)* Visits most probably?

                                JIM

I checked. The only visitor Wesley's had is his lawyer and I know it wasn't him.

                                VAL

So where . . . ?

                                JIM

I don't care who your daddy was. If you're breaking policy . . .

                                VAL

(Genuinely shocked) You're accusing me?

                                JIM

You're the only one.

                                VAL

What the . . . ?

                                JIM

You're a pushover Val.

                                VAL

Just because . . .

                                JIM

You let them get away with anything.

VAL

(Angry) You think I did this?

EILEEN

(Suddenly confessing) Okay. It was me.

Both surprised.

JIM

You?

VAL

What?

EILEEN

I took the letters. I know Amy's aunt.

JIM

(Verbally attacking Eileen) What were you thinking?

VAL

Let her explain.

EILEEN

(A hand on Val's arm) There's nothing to explain.

JIM

(Outraged) You realize you're putting us all at risk. Delivering letters for inmates? I can't believe it.

EILEEN

You're over-reacting.

JIM

Hell I am. Some of us have kids at home.

ACT TWO

EILEEN

I have kids too.

JIM

Well I care about mine.

EILEEN

(Offended) Now you're being insulting.

JIM

My four year old asks every day: When's daddy coming home? I intend to be there for him. Every day.

EILEEN

I assure you. You've got nothing to worry about.

JIM

How do you know? She's talking about coming to visit.

EILEEN

And that's so bad?

JIM

They both know it's never gonna happen.

VAL

That's true, Eileen. They won't let her visit.

EILEEN

Then what's the problem?

JIM

You're so gullible.

VAL

(Attempting to protect Eileen from Jim's anger) Jim.

JIM

They're planning something.

EILEEN

(Dismissively) Really.

JIM

(To Eileen) That would make you an accessory.

VAL

I'm sure Eileen didn't . . .

EILEEN

They're a couple of kids in love.

JIM

(Mockingly) Right. All sweet and innocent. You're a fool. I'm telling Shelly.

VAL

Is that really necessary?

JIM

Yes. It is.

EILEEN

Wesley needs something . . .

JIM

I don't care what Wesley needs. His needs don't override policy.

ACT TWO

EILEEN

(Getting worried) It's just a friendly letter.

VAL

There's no harm been done.

JIM

No harm? You have no idea what could come of this. *(At his wits end)* You've gone too far this time.

VAL

Nothing will come of it. We'll make sure.

JIM

Just see how long your precious programs last.

EILEEN

It has nothing to do with the programs. I take full responsibility.

JIM

I guarantee you . . .

Jim starts walking away, his voice becoming louder as he exits. Val and Eileen stand silent until he's gone through the doors at the end of the corridor.

JIM

Putting us all at risk. Letting them do whatever they want. *(Shouting as he's waiting for the Pshshsht)* Your programs are compromising security.

He exits. Val looks at Eileen. Pause.

VAL

Geez Eileen.

EILEEN

It's just a letter. He's blowing it all out of proportion.

VAL

But if Shelly agrees and they shut down our programs . . .

EILEEN

Âsih *(i.e. "Gee whiz" in Cree)*. I didn't expect him to get hold of the letter. That I regret.

VAL

You can't take anything for granted around here. I tried to tell you . . .

EILEEN

And I told you we'd have to break some eggs. If it comes down to it, I'm prepared to take the hit.

VAL

I don't want that.

Pause.

VAL

You should have talked to me.

EILEEN

That was weeks ago. What does it matter? Wesley was sincere. Mixed up maybe, but sincere. I trusted him then and I still do.

VAL

Maybe you're too trusting.

EILEEN

Too trusting? Listen to yourself. The problem is there's not enough trust. You'll see. These letters are nothing.

VAL

I hope you're right.

EILEEN

I trust those boys more than I trust him *(indicating Jim)*.

VAL

He's the one we have to worry about.

EILEEN

Âs' *(i.e. short for "Gee whiz" in Cree)*. I'm not worried about him either.

They continue down the corridor chatting as they exit.

SCENE 30 - THE RIGHT THING (PERFORMING ESCAPE VI - ESCAPING THE ESCAPE PLAN)

This scene depicts the filming of a videotaped "escape scene" representing Eileen's fantasy – reality and fantasy coming together. Sequentially it occurs some time in the near future, after the events of the play. Eileen is acting in the scene with Randy and Wesley. They have presumably created the scene together under Eileen's direction as part of the Drama program, as part of the Performing Escape sequence. The scene has been rehearsed and is now being staged for videotaping. We see it acted out live on stage and simultaneously we see a video of it projected on screen. Stan is the camera person. He is on stage with a camera videotaping the scene. Eileen is in the scene at all times; sometimes moving closer to or further from the action. Her character interacts physically and verbally with Randy and Wesley; however, while she sees and hears them, they do not see or hear her – ghost-like. Some residual influence of Eileen's presence is at times reflected in the boys' words or actions. The scene takes place in Randy and Wesley's cell. Wesley is lying on the bottom bunk.

(In the original production the Director had the videotaped scene projected on both the TV monitor off to one side of the stage and on the large screen. Eileen, wrapped in the buffalo hide stood by the TV monitor throughout and directed her comments to the image on the TV. The bunk bed, on wheels, was moved centre stage and controlled throughout by the actors playing Val and Jim, one on each end. The bed was moved and spun around as the action progressed with Stan on the video camera following the action shooting close ups.)

STAN

Ready. Action.

The video comes on screen. Randy enters. Eileen enters with him and stays in the background.

WESLEY

(Quietly) Well?

Randy is silent.

WESLEY

(Louder) D'you get it?

ACT TWO

RANDY & EILEEN

(At the same time) Shhh.

WESLEY

(Quieter) Did you?

We see Randy bend over and get something from his sock. He comes up holding up a car key.

RANDY

Ya.

Wesley leaps out of bed, excited.

WESLEY

(Too loudly) Aight dude. You came through! Way ta go.

RANDY & EILEEN

(At the same time – Randy in English, Eileen in Cree). Shut up/Pâkitôn.

Randy looks around anxiously. Wesley gives Randy a big slap on the back.

WESLEY

(Trying to contain his excitement) We're good to go then. Sweet!!!

Wesley goes to sit on his bed. Randy still holds out the key.

RANDY

(Getting Wesley's attention) Wes.

EILEEN

Mîyi *(i.e. "Give it to him" in Cree).*

WESLEY

What?

RANDY

(Holding out the key to him) Here.

WESLEY

What? Put it away.

RANDY

Take it.

EILEEN

Ôtina *(i.e. "Take it" in Cree)*, Wesley.

WESLEY

You.

RANDY

You. I ain't goin'.

WESLEY

Wha'da'you mean?

EILEEN

Îkosi anima *(i.e. "That's the way" in Cree)*, Randy.

RANDY

I decided.

WESLEY

What?

RANDY

It's not worth it man.

ACT TWO

WESLEY

Course it is.

RANDY & EILEEN

(At the same time, Randy in English, Eileen in Cree). No/Mîya.

RANDY

It's not.

WESLEY

Come'on Randy. Man. Can't back out now. It's the plan.

RANDY

(Shoving the key at him) Take it.

Wesley refuses. Randy continues to hold out the key.

EILEEN

That's it Randy.

WESLEY

You gotta.

RANDY

I got it for ya. That's what you wan'ed. But I ain't goin'.

EILEEN

There.

WESLEY

You're in on this man.

RANDY

You c'n go without me.

WESLEY

We're in this together.

RANDY & EILEEN

(At the same time with change of pronoun) It's my/his choice.

WESLEY

That's wack.

Pause. Angrily Wesley snatches the key from Randy's hand and quickly goes and hides it inside his pillow. He begins pacing. Randy sits down on the bed.

WESLEY

(Frustrated) Shithead.

EILEEN

Ow Randy. Pîkis'kwâs *(i.e. "Go ahead Randy. Talk to him" in Cree)*.

RANDY

You know . . .

Wesley is silent.

RANDY

You should f'rget 'bout it too.

EILEEN

Forget about it Wesley.

WESLEY

No way. I'm outta here.

RANDY

Those guys escaped in Regina. They were all awaitin' trial.

ACT TWO

EILEEN

(Nodding her head) Probably looking at life.

RANDY

Lookin' at life prob'ly. It was worth their while to run. But you only got 'nother year. Think about it.

WESLEY

Screw that.

Wesley kicks the bed.

EILEEN

Wesley.

WESLEY

Can't do 'nother year.

RANDY

Think about what'll happen when they catch you.

EILEEN

Mâm'tonîyihta *(i.e. "Think about it" in Cree)*, Wesley.

WESLEY

Shut up. Can't think like that. Gotta stay pos'tive.

RANDY

'Nother charge. Extra time. It'll only get worse.

WESLEY

(Getting angry) Bull. Gotta see Amy.

RANDY

Just think about it.

WESLEY

Said shut up.

EILEEN

Nâkatîyihta *(i.e. "Careful" in Cree)*, Randy. He'll lose his temper.

RANDY

What happens if you do get away? You go into hiding? Where?

WESLEY

(Getting angry) Shut up already. Don't make me hit'cha.

Wesley makes a grab for Randy who retreats to his top bunk.

EILEEN

Kîyâmpi *(i.e. "Settle down" in Cree).*

RANDY

Think they're not gonna find you?

WESLEY

(Angrier) Shut the fuck up.

Wesley goes after Randy trying to pull him off the bed. Randy attempts to kick him away. Eileen tries to break up the fight by pulling Wesley away.

EILEEN

Wesley. Break it up now. Kîyâmpik *(i.e. "Settle down" in Cree).*

RANDY

Quiet.

Wesley gets kicked in the face by Randy's foot after which he gives up afraid of drawing attention from the staff.

Wesley groans. The battle is lost but he's still angry.

ACT TWO

EILEEN

Ow ikos'an'ma *(i.e. "Okay, that's the way" in Cree)*.

WESLEY

(Nursing his face) I got homeys. They'll hide me.

Wesley lies down on his bed.

EILEEN

Ha! Talk some sense into him Randy.

Randy gets down off the top bunk.

RANDY

For how long? How long you gonna run? They're gonna get ya even'chally.

WESLEY

I'll go away somewhere. With Amy. Don't mess this up for me man.

EILEEN

He's trying to help.

RANDY

I'm lookin' out for you.

Pause.

EILEEN

Ow *(i.e. a Cree expression)* go ahead.

RANDY

Before you get into more trouble. Or get someone else in trouble.

WESLEY

Just shut up. Don't give a crap.

RANDY

Don't want more trouble, do you?

WESLEY

Don't care what happens to me.

RANDY

You don' mean that.

Wesley turns away angry.

EILEEN

Go to him.

Randy gets down from his bunk and sits on the bed beside Wesley.

RANDY & EILEEN

It's gonna be okay Wes.

Eileen takes Randy's hand and puts it on Welsey's back. Wesley pushes Randy's hand away.

WESLEY

Get away. Easy for you to say.

RANDY

Goin' through with this plan. It's just gonna cause trouble for everyone. They'll freak if ya try somethin'.

WESLEY

Let'em. I'll be long gone.

RANDY

If ya don't get caught.

WESLEY

If they c'n find me.

Wesley strikes out at Randy and Randy stands up.

RANDY

What about Val 'n Eileen? Don't wanna get them in trouble, right?

EILEEN

You don't, do you?

WESLEY

Don't care about them?

EILEEN

(Reprimand) Maa Wesley.

RANDY

Well they care about you.

WESLEY

Ya, right.

RANDY & EILEEN

They do.

Pause.

EILEEN

Wihtamô *(i.e. "Tell him" in Cree).*

RANDY

Look . . . It was gonna be a su'prise . . . We're planning a sweat. Special for you.

WESLEY

Big deal.

RANDY & EILEEN

(Pleadingly) Wes.

WESLEY

Already got a plan.

RANDY

Forget the plan. It's not gonna work.

WESLEY

You don't know nothin'.

RANDY

Those guys in Regina. They all got caught. Back in jail in a month.

WESLEY

Gotta try.

RANDY

No you don't. I'm tellin' ya. You'll be worse off if you try this.

Pause. Wesley is silent, sulking. Randy moves in closer.

RANDY

Don't see no way out, bro. Just hav'ta do your time. Maybe afterwards things'll get better.

Pause.

WESLEY

(Deflated) 'Nother year.

ACT TWO

RANDY

Val 'n Eileen'll look out for ya.

WESLEY

Screw 'em.

RANDY

They'll help ya get it together.

Pause.

WESLEY

(Sceptical) Sweat lodge ain't even finished.

EILEEN

It will be.

RANDY

Eileen 'n I been workin' on it all week.

Pause.

WESLEY

It's suppos'ta help?

RANDY

For sure it will.

Pause.

WESLEY

What about the key?

Wesley digs for the key in his pillow, finds it and throws it across the room, barely missing Randy.

RANDY & EILEEN

(At the same time, Randy in English, Eileen in Cree) Careful/Pîyahtik.

Randy quickly retrieves the key.

RANDY

What're ya tryin' to do?

Randy jumps back up to his bunk and hides the key in his own pillow. Wesley is silent.

RANDY

I'll give it back to Val tomorrow.

EILEEN

Thank goodness.

RANDY

Eileen says we c'n help with the fire for the sweat.

Wesley rolls over and pulls the covers over him.

WESLEY

Whatever.

Eileen sits on the bed beside Wesley and comforts him while Randy also tucks in to go to sleep.

STAN

Cut.

Stage and screen fade out.

SCENE 31 - INDIAN REBELLION (PERFORMING ESCAPE V - ESCAPING COLONIALISM)

On Athabasca. There are more dreamcatchers and other Native artifacts as well as drawings, etc. around the space. Val, Eileen, Randy and Wesley are standing around watching and listening to Stan beat boxing. Stan is focused and accomplished at creating beats with his mouth. The others are impressed. Stan finishes.

WESLEY

Stan, my man. That is ke-wl!

Stan and Wesley execute a complicated handshake.

VAL

That's really good Stan.

EILEEN

I'll say. Quite a talent.

VAL

(Calling Eileen over to her) Eileen.

Val and Eileen move to one side and start a conversation amongst themselves that we don't hear, while the boys continue talking.

RANDY

Where'd you learn that?

STAN

(Basking in the praise) Just hangin' around the park 'n tryin' it. With some bros.

WESLEY

Sounds sick. Real sick! Com'ere.

Wesley moves to one side of the space, a couple of steps away from where Val and Eileen are conversing and motions for the other boys to follow.

WESLEY

(To Randy) What the word? Talked to Val yet?

RANDY

Workin' on it. Gonna talk to 'er later.

WESLEY

What'cha waitin' for? *(Excitedly)* Have a good feelin' 'bout this.

Wesley and Stan go back to executing other complicated handshakes. Randy stands watching. Eileen, still conversing with Val, calls over to them.

EILEEN

Hey guys. Val and I just need a minute. Why don't you work on another escape scene to show us? Acimostâtok *(i.e. "Tell each other a story" in Cree).*

Eileen goes back to talking with Val. The boys, following Eileen's instructions, prepare to devise an "escape scene" to show. They stand around thinking and exchanging ideas. Stan fiddles with some of the traditional Native clothing pieces around the space. He puts on a quill choker.

WESLEY

That gives me a idea. Astam *(i.e. "Come here" in Cree).*

Wesley motions the other boys into a huddle. We don't hear what they are saying. After a moment they break the huddle each going off in a different direction. Val and Eileen are still talking. Trying not to make their actions too obvious, the boys move around the space collecting items they can wear: a headband with a feather in it, a quill breastplate, the quill choker, a full feather headdress, a hide pouch, a blanket. They bring the items back to the huddle. They take off their T-shirts and begin to dress themselves in the stuff. They chat quietly as they dress, trying to keep their laughter from exploding.

WESLEY

(Motioning Randy to give him the headdress) Gi'me that. I'm the Okimahkân *(i.e. "Chief" in Cree).*

Wesley also takes the blanket and wraps himself in it. Randy dons the breastplate and headband.

167

WESLEY

Here *(Handing Stan the pouch)* for the Windian *(Or Chindian, Blindian, etc. depending on the race of the actor)*.

They huddle again, now all dressed up, devising the details of their scenario and giggling.

WESLEY

(Quietly) 'Kay? Know what to do?

STAN

(In character) Ready great Okimahkân *(i.e. "Chief" in Cree)*. Lead us from this place. *(As himself laughing)* They're gonna have a bird.

RANDY

But be careful.

Wesley chuckles.

WESLEY

(Mocking) Careful. Right. Don't want anyone gettin' hurt.

RANDY

I mean it.

WESLEY

He means it Stan.

STAN

(To Randy) Chill out man. It'll be fun.

The boys creep into position. Eileen and Val finish their conversation and turn towards the boys.

EILEEN

(Curious) What are you guys up to?

As soon as Eileen speaks the three boys spring into action. Wesley begins and the others follow his lead. They all belt out war cries and charge towards the two women. Eileen begins laughing and struggles to get out of their way. Val is startled. She gets caught between Wesley and Randy as they rush past. She stumbles. Randy tries to support her, but Wesley charges into her making it look like an accident. He raises his elbow so as to make contact with Val's nose. Val falls onto the floor holding her nose as the "rebellion" winds down. Wesley quickly moves out of the way. Randy immediately notices Val's distress and goes to help her. Stan and Eileen are laughing heartily. They notice Val on the floor not laughing. They stop laughing too. Val's nose is bleeding. She takes a kleenex from her pocket and applies it to her nose.

EILEEN

What happened?

The boys all looking sheepish – still in their "Indian" garb. Randy looks accusingly at Wesley.

RANDY

Sorry Val. You okay?

STAN

It was a accident. We didn't mean to, did we? *(Looking for confirmation from the other boys.)*

Randy gets Val a chair. Val sits on it. The others stand around.

VAL

(Still covering her nose with the tissue) I'm fine. Just a nosebleed.

RANDY

We're real sorry.

Pause while Val attends to her nose.

EILEEN

Why don't we smudge and call it a day.

Eileen exits to another area of the unit to get the smudge materials ready.

ACT TWO

VAL

(Quietly still holding her nose) I know that little scene was all in good fun . . . But listen. It got a little crazy. You know how that kind of behavior gets interpreted.

STAN

It's supposed to be drama.

VAL

You're right, but we have to keep it in control.

STAN

Was a accident.

VAL

I know. We just have to be more careful, okay? We don't want drama to get cancelled.

RANDY

Won't happen again. Promise. We'll be more careful.

Randy glares at Wesley who has been quiet until now.

WESLEY

Don't know what happened.

VAL

Okay then.

Pause. Silence. Eileen re-enters carrying a shell on which some sage is smouldering. Eileen begins with Val still sitting in her chair. Val smudges. Eileen then goes to Wesley and begins smudging him.

WESLEY

(To Eileen) Did we make our 'scape?

EILEEN

(Eyeing Wesley suspiciously, not sure what to make of the incident) Tikwî *(i.e. "That's for sure" in Cree).*

Eileen turns Wesley around and smudges his back. Eileen then goes to Stan, then Randy, who each smudge in turn.

Fade out.

SCENE 32 - RANDY'S REQUEST

Val's office. Val enters followed by Randy. They are in mid-conversation.

VAL

Sorry the sweat didn't work out for this weekend. We'll do it next weekend for sure. Eileen's arranging for Steven to come on Saturday. Do you and Stan still wanna help with the fire?

RANDY

(Distracted) Sure.

VAL

Thought you'd be more excited. This is what you wanted.

Val motions for Randy to sit down. Both Val and Randy sit.

RANDY

I was hopin' for sooner.

VAL

So you've got something to look forward to for next weekend.

Pause. Randy doesn't answer.

VAL

What's the matter?

RANDY

(Trying to get to his point) Other day . . . The thing with your nose . . .

VAL

I'm fine. It was no big deal.

RANDY

Wasn't a accident.

VAL

What do you mean?

RANDY

Wesley did it on purpose.

VAL

What? Why would he do that?

RANDY

To show me he could.

VAL

Could what? *(Confused and concerned)* What's going on?

RANDY

That's what I's tryin' ta tell ya.

VAL

What?

RANDY

Wesley's losin' it.

VAL

How? What are you talking about?

RANDY

(Still protecting Wesley) Not that he's such a bad guy . . .

VAL

(Losing patience) What's he up to now?

RANDY

Didn't think he'd . . .

VAL

(Coaxing) Randy.

RANDY

To show me he was serious. That he'd really do it.

VAL

Do what?

RANDY

Hurt you.

VAL

Why would he want to hurt me?

RANDY

'Cause . . . he wants somethin' from me.

VAL

What? For heaven's sake. You're not making any sense.

Randy gets up and paces the room, while Val remains seated watching him. Pause.

RANDY

Told ya he's still on about his 'scape plan.

VAL

(Disbelievingly) I talked to him about that and so did Eileen. He promised to drop it.

RANDY

It's for real.

VAL

What? Are you telling me he has a real escape plan?

RANDY

A real plan.

Pause.

VAL

Go on.

RANDY

Him 'n Stan 'n Amy. Thinks he can get out through the air vent into the workshop. And Amy'll help on the outs.

VAL

(Worried now) What? This is worse than I thought. If Shelly gets wind of this. Or Jim.

RANDY

I'm suppos' ta be in on it too.

VAL

You? I thought I could trust you.

Val sits stunned. Randy continues.

RANDY

That's why I'm here. Tried ta talk him outta it. He won't listen . . . My part's the getaway car.

VAL

How are you supposed to get a car?

ACT TWO

RANDY

Your car.

VAL

My car?

RANDY

He said to steal your key. Or maybe you'd give it to me.

VAL

(Disbelievingly) I'm supposed to give you my car key?

RANDY

Said, if I didn't get it he'd hurt you. That's why he did it. I can' let 'im hurt you again.

Pause.

VAL

I'm glad you're telling me this.

RANDY

You are?

VAL

Yes.

RANDY

I'm worried for you both.

VAL

I'm glad you chose to tell me the truth, Randy.

Pause.

RANDY

I know it's crazy.

VAL

When's it supposed to happen?

RANDY

Won't tell me unless I get the key.

VAL

You did the right thing coming to me. We'll figure something out.

Pause. Val is thinking. Randy sits back down.

RANDY

What're you gonna do? Don't wanna get Wes in trouble. He's messed up is all.

Long pause.

VAL

Okay.

Calmly, Val gets up, goes into her desk and takes out her keys. She removes one key from her keychain and replaces the rest. With the car key in her hand she sits back down. Val places the key on the corner of the desk nearest to Randy.

VAL

(To Randy) What are you gonna do?

Pause.

Fade out.

EPILOGUE

Video on screen. (In the original production the epilogue was also projected on the on-stage TV monitor to distinguish it from the video fantasy scenes.) Close up of an anchor person sitting behind a news desk in a studio. We hear the news jingle. A caption on screen says "Crack Down on Youth Crime".

NEWS ANCHOR

In this morning's Safe Edmonton segment we focus on youth crime. And we turn first to the latest from Ottawa.

Switch to video of politician giving a speech.

POLITICIAN

Age is no excuse for crime. Nobody is above the law. We are seeing youth thugs who are committing crimes without fear of consequences. The Conservative Government wants to clean up the youth-crime mess by keeping dangerous youth criminals off the streets while awaiting trial. And through tougher sentences that send a clear message that crime has consequences.

Switch back to news anchor.

NEWS ANCHOR

With us today in the studio we have Sergeant Ron Smith. Sergeant Smith is with Crime Stoppers and a School Resource Officer.

Close up on Sergeant Smith.

SERGEANT SMITH

The increase in youth crime in our city is a real concern. There are plenty of hard working, responsible parents out there whose kids are going off the rails because of a few bad apples in the bunch. Kids are influenced by their peers to get involved in drugs, stealing and fighting and before you know it, they're out of control. We have to teach them before it gets bad that there are negative consequences to their actions.

Switch back to News Anchor.

NEWS ANCHOR

The City of Edmonton and Edmonton Police Services will be hosting a series of community consultation meetings on youth crime over the next several months. Stay tuned for times and locations of meetings in your community. And remember, it takes a community to make Edmonton a safe place to live.

In other news, conclusive evidence that Alberta oilsands are adding toxic compounds to the Athabasca River, damaging to fish eggs and embryos . . .

End of video.

END OF PLAY

CPSIA information can be obtained at www.ICGtesting.com
Printed in the USA
LVOW090834130112

263624LV00002B/1/P